1795

D0457867

Temporary Loan From _____ Main

796.
92

Fraser, Kennedy
Scenes from the fashio-
nable world

17.95

*Also by Kennedy Fraser*


THE FASHIONABLE MIND: REFLECTIONS ON FASHION, 1970–1981

# SCENES
## FROM THE
## FASHIONABLE
# WORLD

# KENNEDY FRASER

# SCENES FROM THE FASHIONABLE WORLD

RICHMOND PUBLIC LIBRARY CALIFORNIA

ALFRED A. KNOPF      NEW YORK 1987

.MAIN
746.92 Fraser, Kennedy
       Scenes from the
       fashionable world 1st
       ed.

31143004139458          c.1

THIS IS A BORZOI BOOK

PUBLISHED BY ALFRED A. KNOPF, INC.

Copyright © 1987 by Kennedy Fraser

All rights reserved under International and Pan-American
Copyright Conventions. Published in the United States by
Alfred A. Knopf, Inc., New York, and simultaneously in Canada
by Random House of Canada Limited, Toronto.
Distributed by Random House, Inc., New York.

All essays in this book first appeared in *The New Yorker*.

Grateful acknowledgment is made to the following for permission
to reprint previously published material:

*Chappell and Co., Inc.:* Excerpt from the song lyrics "Don't
Make Fun of the Fair" by Noel Coward. Copyright 1951 by
Chappell Music Ltd. Copyright renewed. Published in the U.S.
by Chappell and Co., Inc. International copyright secured. All
rights reserved. Used by permission.

The poem on page 33, "Body Is to Spirit," is by Laurance
Wieder. Reprinted by permission of the author.

Library of Congress Cataloging-in-Publication Data

Fraser, Kennedy.
Scenes from the fashionable world.

1. Fashion.  2. Costume designers.  I. Title.
GT511.F72  1987     746.9′2     86-46127
        ISBN 0-394-55483-3

Manufactured in the United States of America
First Edition

FOR MR. SHAWN, WITH LOVE

*I walked up gravely to the window in my dusty black coat, and looking through the glass saw all the world in yellow, blue, and green, running at the ring of pleasure. The old with broken lances, and in helmets that had lost their vizards, the young in armour bright which shone like gold, be-plumed with each gay feather of the east, all—all—tilting at it like fascinated knights in tournaments of yore for fame and love.*

*Laurence Sterne,* A Sentimental Journey, *1768*

# CONTENTS

## AUTHOR'S NOTE

The four short sketches that serve as curtain raisers for this book—grouped as "Scenes from the Fashionable World"—first appeared in 1982 and 1983 in the "Talk of the Town" department of *The New Yorker.* The editorial "we" is an organic element of the "Talk" story as a literary form, and I have chosen to retain the convention for these pages, too. The viewpoint of the vignettes is singular, and the voice, I would hope, my own.

The three longer chapters also appeared first in *The New Yorker:* "The Great Moment" in December 1983, "The Light in the Eye" in December 1984, and "As Gorgeous As It Gets" in September 1986. Fearing to tangle the reader in two kinds of present moment and to risk unbalancing the reality of the stories, I have chosen not to alter their time schemes. The present moment of each chapter remains fixed as that of its initial publication. I apologize to any people who find themselves described here with careers awkwardly frozen in mid-flight.

K.F.
New York, 1986

# SCENES FROM THE
# FASHIONABLE WORLD

---

# A NORMAL TUESDAY

$A$RE you going to the dinner for Erté's ninetieth birthday tonight?"

"This is *such* a big night. I already have two cocktails, a dinner, and a supper."

"Claudette Colbert said she was going, because Erté is a neighbor in Barbados. But from all I hear it's going to be a push."

Today, Tuesday, a lunchtime buzz of voices fills Le Train Bleu, a restaurant that is to all appearances the dining car of a luxurious old European train and is reachable by a set of stairs leading from the sixth-floor housewares department of Bloomingdale's. The double row of white-draped tables set with place cards and champagne *flûtes*, the mahogany window frames giving onto the sky, the velvety green walls and ceiling, like the inside of a pea pod, could just as easily be in an airship as in a train—an airship moored for a moment but set to float off up Third Avenue or over the Queensboro Bridge.

We are sitting at a table with Jerome Zipkin, the man-about-town. He is a shortish man with a barrel chest and a large, egg-shaped head. Whether he is talking—perhaps telling a story about a train, a piece of pound cake, and a butler named Luigi—or sitting temporarily silent with his mouth half open in an ironic ready position, his eyes rake back and forth across the double line of tables stretching the length of the car. People are waving at each other, calling, blowing kisses down the aisle. "Isn't that Sybilla down there?" Mr. Zipkin asks. "I recognize the back of her head."

Countess Consuelo Crespi, sitting opposite him, says there are no Europeans *left* in Europe these days. She knows that they are all in New

*3*

York now because she saw them at a funeral last week. The man beside her, introduced as "Mr. Teddy Millington-Drake, the painter," lights a cigarette.

Zipkin is worrying away at an identity like a terrier with a bone. "You mean the one with black eyes, sitting next to Prince Romanoff?" he says.

White-coated waiters come down the aisle carrying trays of ices shoulder-high. Models follow, carefully avoiding the waiters and casually carrying expensive umbrellas and travelling bags, as though they were on their way to catch a train. A blond man gets up from three tables down and makes his way through as well. "There goes Ash Hawkins," someone says. "I bet he has three more luncheons to go to today."

Zipkin sits squarely facing the table, leaving those who flank him to lean in to his conspiratorial chat. On the starched tablecloth he encounters a woman's hand lying next to his. As he greets people—others in the room are now standing up and stopping beside his table—he massages this feminine wrist with his fingertips, as lightly, rhythmically, and detachedly as if he were stroking a cat. The hand belongs to Arianna Stassinopoulos, a dark-haired young woman with a classic brow and tight coils of braided chignon at her nape. For all her youth, her style of dress and her social manner have that full-fledged, womanly European grandeur. She adores living here, she says. She has a car and driver for this evening to take her to the Erté dinner and some places along the way.

"Cocktails at Derek Granger's, for Anthony Andrews," says Zipkin.

"The opening of the sculpture show for Princess Marina of Greece," says Arianna Stassinopoulos.

"The Erté opening. The Erté dinner. The Bulgari dinner at the Knickerbocker Club," says Zipkin.

"You forgot the Princess Marina supper at Regine's," says Arianna Stassinopoulos.

"There you are," says Zipkin, with a laugh. "Just a normal Tuesday!"

REGALLY upright in posture, in a high-necked purple velvet bodice and galleonlike skirts of purple gazar, Arianna Stassinopoulos opens the door of her apartment. From behind her, a young woman with light-brown wavy hair comes forward, one hand vaguely clutching the soft brocade folds of her fox-trimmed cape. "I'm Arianna's sister, Agapi," she says, giving us her other little hand to shake. "A-g-a-p-i. It's the Greek word for love." We all go downstairs and get into the limousine.

THE Granger party is in an apartment in the fifties near Fifth which turns out to belong to Hardy Amies, dressmaker to the Queen of England. The curtains are drawn. Apart from a motley collection of shells and paperweights on illuminated glass corner shelves; the images of "The CBS Evening News" flickering away, huge and slightly curved, on a giant Advent TV screen; and a signed photograph of Her Majesty in the robes of the Order of the Garter, the room could be that of an expensive hotel in any part of the world. Many of the accents are British. We ask a man with a mustache and a well-tailored suit why the television set is on.

"I think Andrews is starring in a film of *Ivanhoe,* " he says gloomily.

Our host, a small, pixie-faced man in a blue velvet jacket, is the producer of the television version of *Brideshead Revisited,* in which Anthony Andrews plays Lord Sebastian Flyte.

"But where is our *star?* " Derek Granger is asking his other guests. "He must have gone to *sleep* or something."

Above our heads, on the screen, an enormous Dan Rather looms, then the Pope, then a line of black convicts whose jail has just had a bad fire. Arianna Stassinopoulos swims into the thickest of the party with a twitch and a rustle of her panniered skirts. The songwriter Betty Comden, décolleté in black lace in honor of Erté, wonders out loud how she will eat her dinner in elbow-length satin gloves.

"A-g-a-p-i," we hear a familiar voice saying somewhere in the crowd. "It's the Greek word for love."

Andrews arrives and, putting a velvet-clad sleeve around the velvet-clad shoulders of his host, calls him a "sweetie" for hiring the Advent television set, on which (it transpires) he will appear as the Scarlet Pimpernel at any minute. The sisters gather their cloaks, and we all leave —passing under the gaze of the Queen and that of Jerry Zipkin, who is coming through the front door in black tie and boiled shirtfront with a couple of ladies in tow.

OUTSIDE, the evening is turning chill. Agapi Stassinopoulos hastily gathers purse, skirts, and cape folds and fur into one hand and, crouching, ducks into the nearest of a line of waiting cars.

"This ain't your limousine!" roars the driver.

She bundles herself, with some difficulty, into reverse.

AGAPI Stassinopoulos's social route diverges from ours for the next few hours, and her place in the car is taken by a visiting Englishman. He looks bemused as we arrive at Fifty-seventh and Park for the sculpture show of Marina Karella, who is also Princess Michael of Greece. The artist, dressed in red among her creations in bronze or in black plaster, looks bemused, too, as she stands in a crowd which includes some people in tweed coats and hats and some in evening dress. There are a number of young men in amusing bow ties—extra-wide or extra-thin black ones, even one in pink, worn with tails. Prince Michael stands in a quite conventional tuxedo, playing with tasselled black worry beads, or bowing over the hands of women as he tells them about his novel, called *Sultana.* The crowd engulfs Arianna Stassinopoulos completely; then we see her twisting first to one side and then to the other as she greets acquaintances in Greek, answering what seem to be petitions from women who want to make clothes for her or who beg her to grant an interview to some young protégée.

As WE pull away from Fifty-seventh Street to head downtown, there is— silhouetted against a glowing store window containing an antique library globe and a coromandel screen—a lumpy figure with a bedspread over its head, shuffling about in the cold wind and searching through a shapeless bag. In the blue darkness of the back of the car, the occupants lean back and discuss Arianna Stassinopoulos's forthcoming book about the Greek gods. She opens a little evening purse—made, like her pointed slippers, crossed on the carpeted footrest, from the same silk as her gown —and selects from a choice of orderly, minuscule, glittering accessories a lipstick and a compact. As we swing around the right angles of the ramp on the perimeter of the Grand Central building, fingers of yellow light slant into the car from the overhead lamps to modulate and then drown themselves in the purple folds of her skirts.

At ERTÉ'S ninetieth-birthday exhibition and reception in SoHo, he is elaborately placed for observation—a tiny, talismanic person as detailed as a piece of Fabergé, in his soft black leather jacket, black silk socks, and black patent slippers, and seated among a blaze of television lights on a pink silk love seat shaped like Aphrodite's scallop shell. The ample gallery is papered with the brilliant-colored results of Erté's seventy-year career as a graphic artist, illustrator, fashion designer, and creator of sets and costumes for theatrical productions, *spectacles,* and revues. Celebrities inhabiting the contemporary manifestation of Erté's element—many as brilliant-colored as his art—line up to pay him homage. From where he sits on his Lilliputian throne, he lifts up a gold-braceleted hand and a serene yet puckish face, whose blue eyes wear the milky veil of great age. On the sidewalk outside, among the waiting stretch limousines and the parked battered panel trucks, passersby are cupping their eyes with their hands to peer into the bright space and catch a glimpse of Brooke Shields and Halston. Bobby Zarem, the public-relations man, stands looking dazed and nervously fingering his lip. "This is dynamite," he says. "One of the greatest groups assembled in a long time. Almost everybody here is somebody. Of course, they've turned out because it was Diana Vreeland who invited them."

DOWN the block, on the sidewalk outside the restaurant where several hundred somebodies have been invited to dine, palm trees tremble in tubs, and women in thin gowns are shivering in the cold. The crowd is let in through the door at less than a snail's pace while harried attendants check names.

"I can see why Diana Vreeland decided not to come," says a voice.

"This is an outrage," says a second voice.

A handsome youth comes pushing out against the incoming tide, bearing a woman's furs, to leave them in the safety of her car. Erté comes tripping along from the reception on foot and dressed in a mink coat of fitted, feminine cut.

"Oh, Monsewer, Monsewer!" cries one of Zarem's assistants, throwing his hand up and waving madly over the knot of cold and hungry guests. "This way, this way! Oh, please, everybody, stand aside!"

WE SECURE a seat for ourself at last—among what has become a scramble of changed place settings—at a long table at the foot of the dais where Erté sits. Arianna Stassinopoulos, whom we had mislaid at the beginning of the reception, is sitting some places down. Near us sits a man whose hair is brushed straight back and whose expression (after several attempts to catch a waiter's eye) has settled into one of wry yet well-mannered resignation. "Sam Peabody," he says, extending a hand in welcome and relieving himself of an almost imperceptible sigh. "I'm afraid this is turning out to be a rather *difficult* sort of evening." He smiles.

A man sitting opposite stands, pushes back his chair, and ambles off.

"It's because he saw that Gloria was sitting alone," Peabody says with equanimity.

Abandoned thus beside an empty seat, a woman in a high-necked turquoise dress, with an old-fashioned hair style and apparently wearing no makeup, sits staring unhappily down at her asparagus spears.

"Why don't you move down?" Peabody asks. "I think we'd better huddle together, don't you?"

The woman looks at him in blank trepidation, until we discover that she speaks only French, and are able to reissue Peabody's invitation in the language she understands. She is Hélène Martini, and has flown in from Paris on the Concorde specially for the event. She has been a friend and admirer of Erté ever since he dropped into obscurity in the fifties and most people thought he was dead. He has designed many revues for her since then—for her night clubs, which include the two best gypsy *boîtes* in Paris. She tells us that some years ago, as a present to herself on her fortieth birthday, she bought the Folies-Bergère.

A line of spotlights shines down through the room's dim, smoke-filled air, carving narrow triangles of white light and pinpointing shirt-fronts and jewels.

"I have always liked going to bed when the world gets up," says Mme. Martini. "At night, you get to see human beings for what they really are."

The shafts of light are touching the blue-black down of Diana Ross's hair, twinkling on the spangles of her white gown, which is like a show-biz version of a robe for singing in a gospel choir. In all simplicity, she takes the microphone to urge the room to stand and join with her in singing "Happy Birthday, dear Erté." The guest of honor is almost invisible beside the larger bulk of his neighbor at table, Bill Blass. We catch a glimpse of the delicate old face in the light of his birthday-cake candles.

*"Voilà un homme heureux,"* says Mme. Martini, looking at Erté.


ARIANNA Stassinopoulos's newly re-formed group goes on to see what happened to the Princess Michael party at Regine's. On the sidewalk at Park Avenue and Fifty-ninth Street, men in black tie and women in pale furs are getting in and out of limousines and yellow cabs or standing about in distracted groups trying to decide whether to go in, go on, or simply go home to bed. A young woman gets into a cab with a glass of vodka in her hand. Arianna Stassinopoulos, her strength undiminished, sweeps into an upstairs room where dancing is going on and the young men—their wide, narrow, or pink bow ties looking more wilted than when we saw them last—are standing around at the bar. Suddenly, at our elbow, here's Agapi Stassinopoulos again. Jerry Zipkin rounds the corner of the red hall by the cloakroom, his shirtfront as dazzling now as when we saw him several parties back. And here, greeting us like a long-lost relative, is Mr. Teddy Millington-Drake, the painter, whom we first met when the train pulled out a lifetime ago, at lunch.

# LOOKING FOR THEIR PEOPLE

$\bigwedge$s WE left the office one evening last week, the sidewalks were filled with masses of tired-looking men and women moving this way and that. Red and yellow lights coursed round and round marquees; neon arrows flashed on and off. A man sat in the glare of a fast-food shop eating a corn dog. All the way along Forty-second Street, dark shapes stood, and voices hissed, murmured, called out to passersby. "Lovely ladies. Check 'em out," said one voice. "Tapes," said another voice, and "Gold chains" a third. A hooded figure stood guard over a little stack of white cotton socks in cellophane bags. "Toobs," he said over and over, in a mournful bass. "Toobs."

WE HOPPED into an old yellow cab. There was a pool of grubby water under our feet, and the driver made a wrong turn near the spans of the Queensboro Bridge as he tried to find Club A. The white-gloved hands of traffic officers kept waving us on as we circled in the darkness. "You'll have to get out at this corner," said the driver, so we did.

The night club was well filled with one of those jovial, provincial-seeming crowds that will gather whenever a corporation sponsors free drinks after work. In an inner sanctum that was bathed in a strange orange light we found the European designer Karl Lagerfeld, sitting at a table with four extraordinarily handsome young men, finalists in a competition: one of them was about to be judged most handsome of all and awarded the title of National Lagerfeld Man. The actual Lagerfeld has a sternly chiselled Prussian face and wears his hair in a short eighteenth-century-style tuft of ponytail. He sat in silence, only tapping his middle finger on the table from time to time, while the actress Anita Morris, of *Nine,* who was also sitting at the table, pretended to flirt with the handsome young men. She is a woman with an amazing blaze of red hair and an amazing hourglass figure (draped for this occasion in sunflower-colored silk), and the young men, sitting in a close row, looked as cheerful as four birds on a twig. Then they came out before the crowd and sat on four stools in front of a display case filled with pleated golden fans. The jury—Miss Morris, Bill Boggs (the television talk-show host), a *GQ* photographer, and a man from Zoli Models—vanished to reach a verdict on the four. Lagerfeld was now sitting in the front row of tables, wearing dark glasses. A brunette in spangled blue satin entertained, waving one hand like a lasso over her head while belting out "You Light Up My Life." Beside us in the darkness of the audience, two men discussed the finalists.

"I don't know," said one. "His profile is kinda *squashed.* I'll take the one in the pink shirt."

Pink Shirt won, and was to pose for photographs with Lagerfeld and a trophy said to be set with two million dollars' worth of diamonds.

"Where is the trophy, anyway?" Boggs asked into the microphone.

A short man with thinning sandy hair stood up, holding in his hands an odd-shaped, glittering bottle. No one had noticed the man before, and Boggs looked distinctly startled.

"And who are you?" he asked into the microphone. "The armed security guard?"

Everyone laughed.

"I am Buzz Baumgold, of Baumgold Diamonds," the short man said with dignity.

·     ·     ·

WE TOOK a cab to the Metropolitan Museum, where the "Belle Epoque" costume show was to have its gala opening.

At the top of the steps, the doors stood wide, to admit the ball gowns. The Fourth Estate was poised en masse, with hundreds of cameras and notebooks at the ready. Under a house-high profusion of quince blossoms in the Great Hall, young people in period costumes strolled about lending atmosphere. A girl in green silk with an enormous *My Fair Lady* hat paused on the arm of a bowler-hatted youth (who later had to double as a passer of hors d'oeuvres) and scanned the name cards lined up on the seating-arrangement table. "Goody," she said. "All my friends will be here."

Ball gowns were entering thick and fast, and camera flashbulbs were popping. Between entrances, the paparazzi chewed gum, joked, wiped their camera lenses with their handkerchiefs. "I owe you two bucks, O.K.? I got him with his girlfriend, in Washington, and I'm holding out for four thou. A poor turnout that night—only a couple of key shots."

When the key shots came up now—Raquel Welch in python-style sequins, Halston with some women wearing Halstons—the photographers were galvanized into a crouching, jostling semicircle, moving rapidly backward as their subjects advanced. At these moments, they formed a phalanx as irresistible and lethal as a Roman Army unit with swords, shields, and battering rams. We stepped hastily out of the way. Green Silk, parading nearby, trailed her train across the top of our foot; it felt mysteriously dense and soft, like some exotic tail. Then there was a ripping sound, and she whisked furiously round. "Back *off*, won't you?" she said to the bowler-hatted youth, with savagery.

The tableau was almost in place, the gathering almost complete. Men raised their eyebrows at women, with a "What—you here?" sort of look. There were more dress designers, wearing tuxedos, than one would have thought alive. We were dining elsewhere, and didn't have time to wait for the greatest entrance of them all—that of Mrs. Diana Vreeland, as special consultant to the Metropolitan Costume Collection, the organizer of the show. As we headed out and down the museum's great flight of steps, we saw scattered groups of little figures slowly trailing up them, gathering skirts and composing features in preparation for the flashbulbs and the entrances. All along the museum's façade, the fountains, bobbing and dancing with incandescent whiteness, formed a setting for Central Park's horse-drawn cabs, lined up in atmospheric rows, with black silhouettes of nags standing with one fluffy hoof tipped up, waiting and waiting. One of these carriages had a team of drivers—a young man in a chimney sweep's battered top hat and a young woman in a newsboy's white cap—sitting side by side with their feet under a rug on the opposite seat, watching the arrivals. They looked as snug as some old country couple tucked up in bed in a little village in France. They offered to take us on to our dinner, on the other side of the Park, but we declined. The bright-pink mop of Zandra Rhodes' hair was just bobbing out of a cab, and we bobbed into the cab in her place and shut the door. We told the driver, when he asked, that the occasion was the opening of a costume show.

"Some people don't need no costumes," he said, with a nod at Miss Rhodes, who was moving toward the steps.

LATER, a friend we'll call simply Walter came with us to join the crowd at the "Belle Epoque."

"The Belle Epoque should make a nice change," he said. "Modern life I can see any old time."

The scene in the forecourt had been transformed. The horse-drawn cabs had vanished, replaced by rank upon rank of limousines, which had reduced Fifth Avenue to a single lane. Turning to look back from the top of the steps, we saw a sea of jet-black roofs shining in the dancing white fountain light. Several people had had the idea of tying white handker-chiefs to the radio aerials as flags.

The museum's dinner guests were still sequestered in an imitation of Maxim's, hidden at the end of a long, red-carpeted, red-lit corridor containing massive stone sarcophagi. We joined the non-dinner guests milling in the ground-floor costume show.

A baby-faced young man in a tailcoat and in a distinctly after-dinnerish state was looking at the Poirets and the Paquins. "This is nice," he announced. "Whaddisit? Oscar Whazzisname?"

Walter scrutinized the show more critically. "Boldini," he said, peering at a portrait. "Doesn't hold up at all."

People in strange-shaped clothes passed in front of mannequins in strange-shaped clothes, as if parading through a dream.

"I like the stuffed dog," said Walter. "That's a very nice touch."

We went back upstairs, past Egyptian mummies that lay on their backs inside glass cases, staring up at us with painted eyes. The dinner guests were starting to emerge.

They came swimming out of the red light as if on a flood tide—a shoal of famous, well-publicized faces, looking eerily bright-eyed yet calm. The non-dinner crowd formed itself into a human tunnel on either side of the flood and looked on. Down the hall came the famous, passing under the stares of the great stone figures, then (with an almost impercep-tible rearrangement of the mouth, for photographs) humbly exposing themselves to the stares of the living.

"I get it," said Walter. "This is strictly processional. Magic makes kings, after all."

Dr. and Mrs. Henry Kissinger came sweeping out, followed by what looked like bodyguards, then the William Buckleys. The column of dinner guests was gathering force, its ever-denser and faster movement sending the groups on either side swaying at its passage like moored riverboats at the passage of a barge. We could see the famous people talking, but somehow it seemed like an imitation of talk, as though they were extras onstage. The watchers had voices enough for all, though, and a constant murmuring, fluting sound went on around us.

"Did you see those fabulous black transvestites back there?" said one of these disembodied voices, which might have been coming from anywhere—the quince blossoms, the sarcophagi, the walls, the osprey feathers bouncing in the golden curls above some aged face.

"These people don't look as if they're having a very good time," said a voice.

"And I wore this *great* black jumpsuit, with a big pointy collar and studs," said a voice.

"Do you suppose this is *Society*?" said a voice.

Calvin Klein came by on the tide, then women in sculptured silks that gave them lizard shapes, and a series of bosoms rising from sumptuous ceremonial pillows of spangles and feathers. Suddenly, where the tide was at its densest and fastest, we saw Andy Warhol's face, upturned, white as a sheet, being swept along as if it, too, were disembodied.

Walter had stepped away and was standing with his back to the procession, looking into a jewellike corner of the hall. We joined him to look at soft turquoise-and-coral frescoes that glowingly framed a couch and a mosaic floor on which Osiris studied a snake. "I think it's from Pompeii," he said. "This has always been my favorite room."


WE WENT to retrieve our coats. Prominently hung in the checkroom was a floor-length wrap of downy cream-colored fur.

"Is that lynx?" we asked the woman attendant, handing her our check.

"I really couldn't tell you," she said, reaching over to touch it lightly, and looking at it with something very powerful in her eyes. "But that's our *favorite* coat."

We stepped out into the air at last, and suddenly, instead of being among the watchers, we were the watched. A thick crowd of dark-clad men filled the platform at the top of the steps and formed an honor guard down each side. This was an army of drivers, intently searching each face for a client or an employer. Light from the hall behind us bounced off the brass rails and off the shiny plastic peaks of caps. Some limousines way down below us were already beginning to nose out of line like great black alligators, their red rear lights brightly blurred through the bouncing sheaves of fountain light. A wind had got up, and was turning a stray ostrich feather at our feet and thwackingly filling and emptying the banner of the "Belle Epoque" overhead.

We paused at the top of the steps. Peering at the dark-clad men, Walter said, "There is nothing in the world so eagle-eyed as chauffeurs looking for their people."

# DID YOU GET TO MEET THE DUKES?

(Lilting) *Don't make fun of the Festival/Don't make fun of the fair . . . But as they say/The gay display/Means money in the bank.*

—Noël Coward

THE "Britain Salutes New York" arts festival was having its coming out. On the eve of the official debut, we went for drinks to the newly renovated penthouse loft of David Lloyd-Jacob, the New York–based British businessman who dreamed up the whole idea.

"It's the biggest private-sector festival ever held," he said, eyes glowing behind his spectacles. "Excuse me while I pop out and see about this proclamation from the governor." He plunged off across the room through a buzzing, chirping crowd ("How do you do?" . . . "So kind" . . . "Perfectly ghastly" . . . "Terribly sorry" . . . "Absolutely super") whose faces would become as familiar as family portraits in the course of the next days' gatherings.

Mrs. Lloyd-Jacob stood, smiling, in a green heirloom dress. "At first, I thought 'Salute' was an awful idea, but it seems to be a great success so far," she said. "David and I haven't been married very long. We met in the crush bar of Covent Garden, in the interval of *Tristan and Isolde.* Frightfully romantic. Are you musical?"

Sir Paul Wright stood with his wife and daughter. "You really should read the Treaty of 1783," he said.

Lady Wright, the only American-born woman apart from Nancy Astor ever to serve as a British M.P., stabbed a forceful forefinger in the direction of her daughter. "Edited the official program," she said.

"I'd love to talk more," said Jennifer Williams, a London-based American woman with a pudding-basin haircut, who founded the British-American Arts Association. "But I'm late for the Parkinson do at Sotheby's."

"Aha!" we said. "Perhaps you'd care to share a cab?"

THE do was a dinner dance in honor of the very English, Tobago-based photographer Norman Parkinson. *Town & Country* gave it. "That magazine pulls out *some* crowd," said a man watching. "The dresses! The jewels! Did you get a look at Mary Lasker's pearls?" The owners of the dresses and jewels circled near flattering photographs of themselves and told each other that they looked "divine, as always." Invitations— adorned with Parkinson's photograph of the Queen, Princess Margaret, and the Queen Mother (wearing *her* pearls)—had gone out to a selection of the British who were arriving in town to launch "Salute." The tall Mr. Parkinson put his arm round the shoulder of the short Sir Hugh Casson, the president of the Royal Academy, and explained how he'd been able to get the shot of a woman lying on a beach right next to a stallion that was rolling on its back: "I know about horses, you see." Gossip columnists wrote down lists of names; a red-tailcoated toastmaster from London consulted lists on a clipboard and kept things moving along.

At our table, Lord Montagu of Beaulieu said that his business— opening his ancestral home, entertainment park, and vintage-car museum to the public—was up six percent over last year and that he'd just broken the three-pound barrier for admission to such places. "After all, London Zoo is three seventy-five," he said. Between the courses, the dance floor filled with twirling balloons of skirts. Zandra Rhodes, in black chiffon, with fuchsia hair and feathery fishbones of pencilled-in eyebrows (all of her own devising), said she thought that when the Queen opened the Barbican complex, in London, she might at least have worn a crown. Across the table, Koo Stark smiled abstractedly and a man knocked over his wineglass.

"Your Excellencies, Your Graces, My Lords, Ladies and Gentlemen, pray silence," intoned the red-tailcoated man. Each of the gentlemen in the room was about to have a Polaroid camera bestowed upon him as a gift. At the round tables that filled the room, all the faces above black-and-white evening dress were then simultaneously scrunched at one eye and half hidden behind awkward-looking black plastic gadgets that kept whirring and emitting milky-green squares. There was a speech with many quotations from the likes of Shaw and Beerbohm, and a joke about duchesses and ladies. Dukes, earls, and Parkinson thumped the tables at this and bellowed "Order! Order!" The man across the table knocked over his wineglass again.

"YOUR Excellencies, Your Graces, My Lords, Ladies and Gentlemen, pray silence," the red-tailcoated man was saying, and it was the following evening, at the Metropolitan Museum. A large crowd of people had stepped briskly along through rooms hung with Constable paintings in which clouds piled as high as powdered wigs stood in stormy pewter skies. Now the people were milling like extras in the courtyard of the American Wing, before the Palladian-style façade. Members of the Household Cavalry, who had been peering out from lurking places among the Duncan Phyfes, stepped boldly forth in their scarlet coats and plumed brass helmets and let out a mighty trumpet blast from the steps. "Oh, darling, do look at that chubby one on the left," said the Duchess of Marlborough. Someone was smoking a cigar. The Honourable John Jeffry Louis, Jr., the American ambassador to the Court of St. James's, read from a yellow

Western Union slip a message from Nancy Reagan; messages from Prince Charles and Mayor Koch followed. Paul Channon, Britain's minister for the arts (a dark-haired man with high color in his cheeks), said that the festival was important for cultural relations. "And it's going to be tremendous fun," he said.

"So kind" . . . "How do you do?" . . . "Terribly sorry" ran the buzz, through a crowd in which not a few gowns had hems bearing honorable-service marks of at least a decade's Glyndebourne seasons. And lists kept rolling off people's tongues, unfurling themselves like invisible proclamations: lists of organizers; lists of sponsors; lists of titles and celebrities; lists of coming events. One woman even listed the past six British ministers for the arts. "I've worked for all of them," she said. "Counting Norman St. John-Stevas twice." And then there was the lanky man with a toothbrush mustache who listed himself as one of the three men present in kilts. "I am the Master of Glenschee," he told us. "Did you know that almost all the tartans had to be reinvented by a Polish tailor named Sobieski Stuart?"

"Contemporary Britain also wishes to salute," said Lyon Roussel, of the British Council, the government-funded organization that has supported some of the festival's newer art forms. "It's easy enough to get corporate sponsorship for something like the Constable show." He caught the arm of a man who was passing by. "What do you recommend among the more experimental things, Hugh? Hesitate & Demonstrate?"

"Hesitate & Demonstrate," said the man. "Definitely."


"DEAR old Queen Mary, she did have this tiny tendency to expropriate things that caught her fancy from other people's country-house bedrooms."

"Lovely island, that. Inland, of course, not the coast. Pity they don't believe in drains."

After many more dinners, parties, receptions, over several more days, some of the British visitors were looking a little the worse for wear. There were subversive thoughts of hotel-bedroom suppers in front of the TV.

"They're not used to the New York pace," Mr. Lloyd-Jacob said when we saw him at a tea party in Bloomingdale's. "And, of course, for these few weeks in spring there's a six-hour time difference, and that makes it considerably harder to adjust."

Ambassador Louis gave a party at the United States Mission to the United Nations, and there was a red double-decker bus parked outside. "My daughter had to go to Los Angeles," Lady Wright told us. "Her daughter is marrying into a doughnut fortune."

The Master of Glenschee, in a gray flannel suit with watch chain and red carnation, hailed a man from the London Embassy. "What ever happened to old Bob Feathers?" he asked.

"He moved on," said the other. "But the tea lady still thinks I'm him."

Sir Hugh Casson was there, an animated figure in black-framed spectacles, holding court under the branches of an indoor tree. "Such fantastic enterprise and *zip* here," he said. "Patronage as well as talent. And a give-it-a-whirl sort of attitude that's wonderful for artists."

"Goin' on? Care to share a cab?"


AT THE Trump Tower, the doormen in their busbies had left for the day, and the grand piano in the rose-pink marble hall was shrouded. But sounds of chatter bouncingly echoed from the second-floor balcony, where Asprey, the expensive London gift store, was giving its "Salute" party in its new premises, for the benefit of the Royal Oak Foundation. The Dukes of Marlborough and Wellington were there, moving as easily through the little gathering as they would among their tenantry at home. Sir Hugh

Casson was already ensconced at the center of a group of ladies who were as ornamental as some of the rare silver pieces that filled the display cases at his back. A man from Asprey waved at the priceless things from churches and Elizabethan manors. "These have never left England before," he said. "They have never even been to *France.*" Then he led us up to an enormous modern replica of the American bald eagle which was made of jagged, glistening rock crystal with solid-gold head, beak, and claws. There was a snowy owl made of crystal, too, and it stood fixing us with its piercing amber eye. "It says 'Don't touch,' " the man said. "But you may." We laid a finger on its eerie furry trouser leg. Then the man pointed at a stack of fitted wicker boxes on the floor. "Our picnic baskets," he said. "We're famous for those."

A very young man in black tie was listening to an elderly man talk about a club founded six years before the Revolutionary War and at the same time was making arrangements with a young Englishwoman with punk blond spikes of hair and a black miniskirt. "I can't leave early. I'll be there by midnight, if I can." The youth was Edwina Sandys' son and Winston Churchill's great-grandson; like his kinsman the Duke of Marlborough, he had a small-chinned face with unusual oval eyes. A portly man in a red eighteenth-century coat and knee breeches suddenly leaned his ruddy, perspiring face close enough to ours to tickle it with the ostrich feathers that dangled from his three-cornered hat. "I'm London's Town Crier," he said, blowing the feathers out of the way with a practiced huff. "I was there to do the old Oyez, Oyez for Prince William's birth, but mostly I'm off hard-selling London all over the world. Budapest; the Philippines; Walt Disney World; parachute out of a helicopter; Citywide Treasure Hunt kickoff in Central Park in a 1907 Rolls-Royce. Camel down Kensington High Street. His Holiness the Pope."

Arthur Prager, the executive director of the Royal Oak, came up and took us away. "I can't think how he got in," he said. "And that awful crasher who calls himself a Spanish count is here as well. Did you get to meet the dukes? Have some champagne. Laurent Perrier, trying to break into the Dom Pérignon market. Wellington posed for a photograph with it. He's very good about that sort of thing."


DOWN at Franklin Furnace, an experimental-performance-art space in TriBeCa, we talked to some British artists.

"What does being British mean, anyway?" said one. "Is nationality something that can be imposed on you from the outside? This whole thing started as a dream, a context for art, and it's ended as a corporate promotion—using artists to sell more whiskey."

"I'm more detached," said a second observer. "It's just that Britain is complex and P.R. can't be."

This subdivision of "Britain Salutes New York" was brought to order not by any toastmaster but by a youth in a mesh baseball cap, holding a beer bottle at his thigh. "Yo," he said, and gave a loud whistle to silence the young artists who were standing around talking, leaning against pillars and walls. "*Soundworks,* by Gerald Newman and Stuart Brisley. Starts downstairs in one minute."

We went down rumbling wood stairs into a basement-smelling space with folding metal chairs. The lights faded, then were turned off completely, and we sat in utter blackness listening to mystic electronic clicks and poetic utterances about the Falklands, the Royal Wedding–street riots summer, nuclear waste. Our eyes felt smoothed and soothed, wide open in the dark. A dark silhouette beside us in the room spoke up in a British voice: "Of course, this work is very visual."

# MAGIC

---

$A$T a viewing of Dakota Jackson's furniture designs, we stood at his side before his neoclassical credenza. A round crystal vase held clear water, pierced at a slant by the stems of pale-colored orchid spikes. Flowers, vase, water floated on a rectangle of heavy glass, in cross-section as green as the sea. Our gaze went snorkelling on down to the substructure: an arch of tinted leather, columns of rich veneer. "It's like a pheasant under glass, I think," said Jackson. He is a tall, slim, high-cheekboned man with a distinctive, catlike physical presence. We followed him into an adjacent room. "This is my earlier work," he said. "My idea of subtle tension. Furniture as deadly weapon." He leaned over a coffee table made of several heavy discs and fan blades of glass, pivoted one above another on a central column. Gently placing the pads of his splayed fingers on the limpid surfaces, he sent them slowly, concentrically circling, like the celestial spheres. "I'm the only one who gets to do this," he said. "It's not meant to be moved."

Diane Von Furstenberg, the designer, invited people to a supper later, in Mr. Jackson's honor. We went into her bedroom to see her bed, which Mr. Jackson created for her some years ago. It is large, astounding, sumptuous, with sunbursts of cherry wood and quilted ivory satin at head and foot. The room's walls were papered with a swarm of full-blown pink cabbage roses and hung with large Victorian oil paintings of maidens in various stages of undress. From high above the bed, a pink-and-white reclining nude gazed down impassively at a little group of people standing chatting round the footboard. There was a tall man with gray hair and the same aura of stillness as Dakota Jackson: his father. A woman chic, as for a wedding, in black-and-white silk, with a rakishly angled large-brimmed hat of shiny black straw: Jackson's mother. And a man with gold-wire glasses, freckled bald head, a double-breasted dark suit as proper as a Victorian undertaker's introduced to us as Dr. Bernard Ackerman.

Carrying a plate of food, we went to sit in the drawing room.

"We dreamed about a lion last night," we remarked to Laurie Anderson, the performance artist.

"Ah!" she said, leaning closer with her funny spikes of close-cropped hair. "Did it have . . ." With her hands, she sketched around her small, expressive face pouchy cheeks, pointed ears, an abracadabra whoosh of whiskers. "Was it, like, a *real* lion, or a *mask*?"

This room, too, was hung with Royal Academicians' canvases—these of epic scenes and allegorical slave girls. Below, next to potted palms, people sat eating back to back on round Victorian banquettes of buttoned velvet. Dakota Jackson stood close beside his wife at the entrance from the foyer, watching guests and apparently thinking, index finger to lip. His father was standing beside a bronze statue, drink in hand, and when he saw us approach he set down his glass. He slid his hand into his jacket pocket and pulled out a sheaf of cut-up Citibank brochures. There was a flip and a rustling sound, and he had turned them into a bouquet of crisp twenty-dollar bills.

"Good heavens!" we said.

"And I served a magician's apprenticeship with my father," said Dakota Jackson, materializing at our elbow.

The older man handed us his professional card. "Thaumaturgist," it read, and gave an address in Middle Village, New York. "I come from a theatre and variety family," he said. "My sister was a Talking Woman. My father was a song-and-dance man."

He asked us to lay two fingers on his wrist, and we did. "Watch very closely, now," he said. A silver dollar blinked and vanished, but not, we swear, up his cuff.

"My early designs were all about hidden compartments," said Dakota Jackson. "Even with the new things, there's illusion, surprise, the idea of the conjurer's wand."

In the bedroom corridor behind the father and son, a coatrack held strangers' garments, waiting passively, square-shouldered in the shadows, nestled chest to back. Diane Von Furstenberg, with her wild cloud of russet hair, came clickety-clacketing in high heels down the hall, in her wake an Indian file of European friends all talking at once in foreign languages.

Dakota Jackson's mother, in her big black hat, was eating dessert —a salad with little pieces of bright-colored fruit. "I help my husband with the act," she said, "but only when we're out at sea."

"There's Jack Nicholson in the doorway, with his arm in a sling," said Dakota Jackson's wife, looking past our shoulder. "Now he's gone again."

Some of the guests ate supper in the bedroom, sitting on hassocks on the floor against the foot of the bed, as if they were warming their backs by a stove. The apartment windows, draped in tasselled curves of silk, gave on to a pale-navy sky, the twinkling lozenge lights of Central Park, a full and haloed moon.

The man with the freckled head came up and made a sort of bow over Mrs. Dakota Jackson's hand. "Good night, Dr. Ackerman," she said, adding as he retreated, "He's the skin pathologist, you know, who testified in the Jean Harris case." She held her palm toward us as if halting traffic, then pointed at it to mark the trace of an imaginary bullet.

# THE GREAT MOMENT

———————————

IT HAD been one of those New York days when the Hudson River gives off a smell of Maxwell House and sea. It was early November, 1982; muggy as could be; just getting properly dark. Two thousand people gathered on the pier beneath the U.S.S. *Intrepid,* waiting to board and attend a fashion show by the Japanese designer Issey Miyake. From stem to stern, the aircraft carrier–turned–museum was bathed by floodlights in a rose-pink glow. The great prow loomed way above the waiting people, like some cumbrous giant of a flamingo coming in to land. There was an excited brandishing of yellow invitation cards, the bark of a bullhorn or two. There would have been helicopters hovering overhead, and shedding beams of light on decks that long-forgotten kamikazes used to swoop at, but low clouds had put paid to that extra touch. Lines of little black figures now moved across the gathering gloom of the pier and began to trail up a zigzag metal staircase on the ship's pink flank and disappear inside a lighted opening halfway up. The instant of guest meeting brilliance was in many cases striking: there were heads with hair like colored paint-brushes or Rastafarian snakes; shoulders twice as wide as life; taut leopard skin–covered thighs; a shoulder blade bright with a dragon breathing fire. Suddenly, at my elbow I found Barbara Weiser.

"Gracious!" she said. "I never thought we'd actually find each other, in this mob. Jon and my mother are supposed to be in there somewhere."

Selma Weiser and her son and daughter, Jon and Barbara (both in their thirties), are the proprietors of a handful of Charivari stores, for men's and women's fashions, on the Upper West Side of Manhattan. Inside the ship, Barbara Weiser and I stood in the jam-packed crowd in front of massive closed fire doors that were like something out of *The Guns of Navarone.* Strangers were telling other strangers behind them not to *push.* Barbara Weiser, back from the latest of an endless round of buying trips to Europe, said that the fashion shows in Paris were just too crazy now. "It's like being an electrified rat, day after day," she said, demonstrating with shoulders up and arms held rigid by her sides. Her eyes, wearing gleaming pewter-colored eyeshadow, popped open in mock pain; her brows disappeared from view beneath bangs of a cap of dark hair. To the right and left of the impatient crowd (whose collective breath was hot and sweet with cognac, for Rémy Martin had provided not only the money for the rose-pink lights outside the ship but also a bar, inside) were roped-off areas in which vintage biplanes were parked. The great metal doors slid slowly open at last, and we all moved, as if sucked in by a vacuum, into a space where, under a ceiling that writhed with engine-room boiler pipes, there was a runway and an army of chairs.

Selma Weiser half turned in her seat and waved her program at us. She was a noticeable figure, with fiery-red hair cut in a cap like her daughter's. Her form, more ample than Barbara Weiser's, was, like hers, draped for the occasion in the fashions of Issey Miyake. "I noticed that some people had little red stars on their tickets," she said, removing bag, shawl, and umbrella from two seats she had saved at her side. "I'd like to know what, exactly, qualifies you as a V.I.P. around here if people doing our kind of business don't make the grade." A generally benevolent indignation is one of Selma Weiser's most frequent modes, coexisting closely with a fierce enthusiasm. She is an indefatigable traveller and improviser in foreign tongues; a hard-nosed bargainer; a great tilter at windmills and follower of hunches; and a brilliant tactician in obtaining unobtainable invitations, reservations, or plates of buffet food. The fashion business suits her.

I studied the program. It was a large white folded card with some

remarks by Miyake on the back and on the front a poem (by Laurance
Wieder), reading, on the left side of the page:

> Body is to spirit
> As cloth is to body
> Grown to its own size:
> Room in the air.
> Air in the weave.
> Waves in the breeze.
> The earth spins and
> Things come to an end.
> So, day and night,
> A body blooms
> At its own hour.
> Stretch the pause
> Through the sky,
> Or float—muted banner—
> Signs, no designs.

On the right side of the page was the same message, the lines backward
—starting off, that is, with the signs that were not designs; pivoting on
an earth that was waving in the breeze; and ending with "Body is to
spirit." In the center of the folded card was a double-page photograph of
the New York postmodern dancer-choreographer Trisha Brown. A handsome woman in her late forties, with large, haunted-looking eyes, she was
standing with one arm raised at a right angle to her body as if to summon
up something or ward off a blow. She wore an unassuming, loose-cut
cotton garment with rolled sleeves and sashed in traditional Japanese
style. At the far end of the runway, light glowed suddenly blue. Members
of the New York Choral Society were standing at the top of a flight of

steps—men and women, singing away, dressed in more of the loose cotton garments, which were from Miyake's new Plantation line. Then models mounted a second flight of steps, behind, stood silhouetted at the top, and came down. Wave after wave of very tall, very thin women, some white, some black, some Japanese, swayed their insectlike hips on their insect-like legs as they sailed downstairs and moved down the runway in fluidly floomph-floomphing lengths of cloth.

"Here come the flying-squirrel things," Barbara Weiser said. "You can put your arms and legs into any combination of the openings."

Colors changed, glowed, faded on the background wall; strands of music flowed; sets of heads repeatedly passed and then retreated, in hats of bamboo like the spread tails of peacocks, hats of cloth like the ears of elephants, hats made of recycled egg cartons and shaped like sat-on Stetsons. A very long-necked, small-faced black woman came by on high-arched feet, the first time walking with her childish arms moving behind her back like parallel pendulums as she shimmied and rattled her bangles in a tufted flapper dress, to music filled with jungle calls. Next, she was undulating and preening inside a waterfall of white silk fringes, with what looked like ceremonial tribal fly whisks sticking out from her shoulders. Then, arching her neck, her hands, her back, her feet, she was walking by in an amazing molded bathing suit.

"I heard he was influenced by Ansel Adams's Yosemite book," Barbara Weiser said, arranging her own Miyake draperies about her and rising to applaud a slight, dark-haired man, dressed in black, who had come out among the models to smile, bow, and raise his eyebrows in happy recognition of acquaintances in the first row.

Outside the ship, it had started to rain. Slanting lines of vivid dot-and-dash drops were tinged by the floodlights, which had been switched to green while we were sequestered in the bowels of the *Intrepid*. Selma Weiser opened her umbrella, arranged her shawl, marshalled her

34

group toward a small dry space, and dispatched Andy Maag, a tall blond man, who was Jon Weiser's assistant, for her son's car. Mr. Tomio Taki, head of Takihyo, Inc., and Mr. Koichi Tsukamoto, head of the Wacoal Corporation, had kindly sent each of us an invitation to a buffet dinner for Issey Miyake at the Mr. Chow restaurant, on East Fifty-seventh Street. I got in the back of the car with Selma Weiser and with Sheila Bernstein, of the Associated Merchandising Corporation. Next to Andy Maag, who was in the driver's seat, Barbara Weiser sat on the knees of her brother, Jon—a broad-shouldered, dark-haired man who bears some resemblance to Dustin Hoffman as well as to his mother and sister.

"Isn't that Mary Russell, from *Vogue*?" said Selma Weiser, scanning the crowd on the pier.

"Mo*ther*," Barbara Weiser said, her voice strangled because her head was pressed up against the ceiling. "We don't have *room*."

In the striped green light of the pier, pale Japanese faces were bowed into stretch limousines. We pulled out among the shadowy puddled potholes under the old, dead highway. There was the Brushless Car Wash —a low structure covered with a brilliant-colored mosaic of pulsating, circus-spangled fountains. Jon Weiser swivelled his head to peer up through the windshield at this mysterious and flashy tunnel. "I never noticed that before," he said.

Two hundred invited guests and some who weren't invited milled around at Mr. Chow. How would we all get fed? Issey Miyake, in a change of clothes—sand-color—appeared on the balcony by the door. Everyone applauded. He circled the room, shaking hands. His mobile face lit up with greetings, his forehead rumpled with amazement and delight. He was telling Barbara Weiser about fitting the chorus in his Plantation line. "Same size clothing, men from six foot four to women five foot—ordinary people," he was saying, rolling up from his forearms imaginary garments, to show the only adjustments to be made.

Yutaka Tada, a tall man with graying hair and a drooping brindled mustache, who is the president of Issey Miyake International, told Barbara Weiser he was tired. "People from Bloomingdale's came in. People from Israel. People from Satellite Communications," he said.

Selma Weiser said to no one in particular that she was dog-tired herself. She found places at a big, round table in a corner of the restaurant and leaned an elbow on the cloth. "We were three weeks in Paris, three in Italy before that. Now we've got to turn around and do Tokyo as well."

The Weisers sat with plates, discussing Mr. Chow's shrimp. Andy Maag knelt on one knee, like a spear carrier, and used the other knee as a table. There was constant movement as people went to or from the buffet or left for home. A newspaperwoman took notes while Barbara Weiser explained why fashions from Japan were the only really interesting fashions in the world at that moment. "It's their whole aesthetic," she was saying. "Their interest in form."

Three newcomers arrived to take up empty places at the corner table. Grace Jones, the singer and "personality," wore Miyake's famous particolored wing-shoulder vest made of wetsuit rubber, with his broad-brimmed padre hat. Bethann Hardison, the model, was all in Miyake red, with a golfer's red peaked cap. André Leon Talley, the fashion writer, was in a sartorial scheme all his own, with a flat-top haircut, a cowboy neckerchief, and a purse like a plaid vinyl toilet kit tucked under one arm. All three were black; they all seemed imposingly tall as well.

A woman wearing a jacket with great fluted silk sleeves like puffs of meringue made an entrance and headed across to the table through the crowded room.

"Daniela!" shouted Talley, as if it were a scene in a play they had rehearsed. He helped her to remove the meringues and left her exposed in a snappered top that kept falling off one shoulder. "Oh, come on, now," she said to him mock-reprovingly in an Italian accent, tugging at the top and looking at herself in the smoked mirror covering the walls. She had a wild white face and wild black hair and a beauty spot on one cheek. She perched herself on Talley's knee.

Then Iman Haywood, the black model who had shimmied, moved her arms like pendulums, and arched her feet, slid in to a place at the table, too. Peter Beard, the photographer, was suddenly there in a dinner jacket, ferociously applying himself to a plate of food. "I brought her from Somalia, you know," he said to me, pulling Iman toward him while he went on eating. She curled closer, resting a thin brown hand on his white shirtfront. "I could see right away she was *great,*" he said. "That beautiful, unspoiled body. The *authentic* African. She could *walk,* you know." He gave a sigh.


ON THE sidewalk, Selma Weiser was somewhat revived. When we left, Talley had been saying to Iman and to Grace Jones, "Let's go out! You have to work tomorrow? How about you? Do let's go *out!*"

"We had the best table of all, in the end," Selma Weiser said. "That girl is simply beautiful. Did you happen to notice her teeth?"

Sheila Bernstein, who was leaving for Tokyo in the morning, still had quite a bit of packing left to do. "Teeth you can buy," she said.


WHEN I arrived in Tokyo, a couple of weeks later, I went to lunch with Hanae Mori. I was escorted in a cab from the Hotel Okura by Carl Morton, the fashion director of Hanae Mori USA, who happened to be in Tokyo at the time. He had a light-colored mustache, a serious and diplomatic manner, and a funny, fashionable suit with chalk-striped pants which was like a pastiche of a Harrods floorwalker's. "Madame Mori is a gentle and sophisticated woman," he said in the cab.

The restaurant called L'Orangerie, one of many things owned by my hostess, was on the top floor of her headquarters—a brittle, angular modern edifice of reflecting glass shaped like a squared-off version of a butterfly. On butterfly wings, printed or hand-painted in expensive, conservative fashion designs, Mme. Mori has fluttered to a position of immense wealth and broadly based power.

"Nouvelle cuisine," Madame said as we sat down with Morton and her chic, Parisian-seeming right-hand woman, Yasuko Suita. "The chef is perfect." Mme. Mori was dressed all in black, with owlish tinted glasses. She had the old-style Japanese feminine voice—birdlike and soft—and she was much given to thoughtful humming sounds. "Everyone is interested in fashion," she said. "Even the gentlemen and the political people."

The elder of her two sons, Akira Mori, is the editor and assistant publisher of *Women's Wear Daily for Japan*. Over the past several years, Mme. Mori and Akira had organized shows by Western and Japanese designers—actually, a series of individual shows launched by a gala evening and group show—in The Space, an area across the hallway from where we sat. *Women's Wear Daily* in New York had regularly covered these faraway presentations, which had brought about sometimes improbable-sounding juxtapositions of internationally known designers.

"The shows worked well to promote Japanese fashion power," Mme. Mori told me. "Kicked off communication. Young Japanese designers came to learn. Karl Lagerfeld and Perry Ellis developed business here after their trips. This year, Norma Kamali, Sonia Rykiel, Valentino, Kansai, Hanae Mori. Next year, who knows?" (Miyake, who was busy planning a multimedia international exhibition as well as his regular, next-season collection, and whose long-standing relations with Hanae Mori were in a period of some friction, had withdrawn from her group event, and would attend only as a guest and an observer.) Mme. Mori now invited me to attend what were billed as the "Best Five" fashion shows and the opening-night party. "Fifty-five ambassadors and their wives," she said. "And royalty. Princess Hanako Hitachi. Very fashion-conscious young lady."

While I sat trying to reconcile all this with the idea of "Japanese fashion" which had in recent months been exciting fashionable people in the West—surreal, postapocalyptic assemblies of inky rags; irrational, anarchic shapes and punctured fabrics; heads of unruly hair tied up in bags; feet in shoes like sea urchins or retreat-from-Moscow twists of cloth —Mme. Mori and Miss Suita were engaged in that most Japanese of activities, consulting each other. Then Mme. Mori hummed.

Miss Suita spoke up. "Why are you all focussing on us now?" she asked, with feeling. "Why so many eyes on Japanese fashion now? We have been the same way for a long time. This is too fast. Too much. Like a *fever*. Why are you *here*?"

The question hung between us as I thanked Mme. Mori for the lunch. She told me to get in touch with Miss Suita if I needed any help in Tokyo. "I can do anything here," Hanae Mori said.


WHILE I was in Japan, it was the wedding season. As I sat in the lobby of the Okura waiting for Yutaka Tada, the Miyake firm's president, to escort me to the hot springs at Atami, female wedding guests in full kimono flitted and scampered by in front of a great paper-screen window. Silhouettes of obi bumps and slanting ornamental hairpins were etched against the checkered, pearly luminosity. Male wedding guests strolled through the lobby in groups—prosperous, solid figures, as compact as rolled-up rugs, wearing identical silver neckties and carrying identical pink paper shopping bags. Tada and I were driven to the Tokyo railway station. As we walked along the platform, he walked a half pace ahead. To left and right, the towering blue-and-white snouts of *shinkansen,* the high-speed trains, slid in and out like clockwork sharks. When Tada was settled in his seat, with his stocking feet on the carpeted footrest, I passed along Miss Suita's question. Why was Japanese fashion getting such attention in the West?

"French, Italian, American fashion very quiet right now," he answered smoothly. "Japanese talent very fresh-looking."

I brought up the paradox that Japanese fashion was seen abroad as original and individualistic, while Japanese society seemed concerned with imitation and groups.

"The market for fashion is very young here," he said. "After they marry, tastes become more conservative. This is a small country—we are thinking always of our neighbor. No real concept of individualism here. My daughter wants to visit New York; she is nineteen. But I say she is used to groups, not ready yet for individuals, like in New York."

THE faces of four individuals turned to look up as Tada and I ducked and entered the upstairs room at the traditional-style inn in Atami. The individuals, sitting or kneeling at a low table on the tatami matting, had been blended into something like a group by uniform wraps of blue-and-white cotton, provided to all overnight guests. I stowed my clothes and, in a similar kimono, lowered myself to the table.

"We've already been to the bath," said Mary Russell, fashion-news director of American *Vogue,* an athletic-looking woman with cropped hair, setting down her tiny teacup. "It's too dark to see now, but it's down that cliff."

"The water is so good for the skin," said Barbara McKibbin, executive editor of *Vogue*.

Joyce Ma, who owns fashion stores in Hong Kong and homes in Rome, London, and New York as well as in Hong Kong, bent her birdlike head of flat, slicked blue-black hair and rubbed red-nailed fingers appreciatively along the skin of her forearm. Tada, now also dressed in a blue-and-white cotton wrap, slid a screen shut behind him and came to sit with us. Makiko Minagawa, whom Tada had described on the train as Issey Miyake's "strong right hand" as well as his textile designer, had been watching the visitors with a little smile. She now pushed back her kimono sleeve with a graceful movement and poured *sake* into Tada's cup.

The banquet began. With deft accordion-unfoldings of kimonoed knees, the chambermaid moved around the table serving and clearing course after course of dollhouse-sized platters and covered dishes.

Mary Russell lifted the lid from a dish and photographed the contents. "You have to be *in* Japan to experience Japanese fashion," she said, taking up her chopsticks again.

"It's like a jewel," Joyce Ma said, looking at her sashimi and sighing. "You can see meanings everywhere."

Tada poured himself some Sapporo beer. The proprietress of the inn, an exquisite little silk-clad personage as finely detailed as her premises, was kneeling in the doorway with her forehead bowed over hands folded on the tatami. Then she was smiling and nodding at this group of visiting foreign businessmen who were somehow all women. She was musically conversing with Tada and Makiko Minagawa. She was somehow at my elbow, speaking in whispers, apparently to let me know that the delicacy I sipped was made with chrysanthemum petals. She was bowing and bowing, and then, in a cloud of pattering compliments for her cuisine, her obi accessories, her pale-powdered complexion, she had vanished. Tada (whom Joyce Ma addressed as Tada-san, in imitation of the Japanese) told a gourmet-misadventure story about a hundred-and-fifty-dollar fish. Then, after exchanging laughing remarks with Makiko Minagawa, apparently about the eccentricities of *gaijin,* or foreigners, he let his attention to the conversation drift.

Mary Russell was talking about Japan's pickle shops. "The long, thin, skinny ones next to the fat ones, the crinkled ones, the pink ones, and the purple kind—those pickles are so *chic*! You can see fashion all around you if you have an eye."

"That's true," Joyce Ma said, holding a chopstick at arm's length and squinting along it like a painter. "You could see fashion in one half of Tada-san's mustache if you wanted."

Tada, by now thoroughly somnolent, jumped. He put three fingers over his mustache, protectively. The maid looked round the table from one face to another, trying to understand.


WE FIVE women, looking in our uniforms something like Buddhist monks, stood reflexively bowing and bowing after Tada-san as he backed out and retired to his room for the night. Housemen arrived to remove the table and replace it with five futons. A conversation about Madison Avenue meat markets trickled along as faces were moonily massaged in circular motions with cold cream. On the balcony, Makiko Minagawa sat smoking a cigarette. There was a sound of cicadas and of waves on the rocks far below; murmurs and giggles could just be discerned from the rooms around.

I thought of fellow-guests, both men and women, coming to soak themselves in the beneficial waters of the common bath, and said that the notion of modesty must be different here.

"Everyone has a body," Makiko Minagawa said, by way of reply. She made a gesture with her palm, as if veiling forehead and eyes. "It is the spiritual you keep secret, the things of the mind."

.   .   .

A SHIATSU masseuse, earlier ordered up by the women who were now soundly sleeping in the darkened room, turned to me instead and dispatched me into sleep as well, with her ministrations to back, knuckles, and soles of the feet. After the brief, hallucinatory rest of the jet-lagged first-time visitor to Japan, my eyelids popped open again, and it was dawn. At the level of my gaze, in front of the balcony window, was a round basket piled with oranges—gleaming, luminous spheres, each with a set of glossy dark-green leaves. The wide window opening was like a double proscenium—the closer formed by the pushed-back white paper screens, the outer by sculptured swags of pendulous tree branches in the garden. Inside this frame was stretched a gray silk, faintly steaming sea that seemed lit from below, like a translucent dance floor. Fishing boats—with both smokestacks and triangular sails, and with tiny men in silhouette— skimmed over the surface to nets whose floats lay necklacelike in curves and angles, marking off their undersea frontiers. Conical volcanic mountains, each a paler shade of gray than its nearer neighbor, marched single file into the distance around the curling coast. In the sky, a giant watercolor brush had left a single stroke of rosy mauve, and a huge black cormorant slowly wheeled.

JOYCE Ma, the women from *Vogue,* and I went clattering in wooden pattens down through the monkey-puzzle trees to the bathhouse at the bottom of the hill. We paused to exchange group bows with a company of Japanese women returning, all with giant pastel plastic bobby pins in their black hair and with towels over their identically robed arms. A second group of women was in the wooden pavilion, first crouching, pale-haunched, on a line of little wooden stools, to wash in little wooden buckets, then stepping into the warm green waters of a rectangular stone pool. Seeming enormously tall—the more so because we had twisted white towels like busbies round our heads—our party followed suit.

"I envy you," Mary Russell said, turning her turbanned head to me as we sat with our shoulders emerging from the bath. I had told her I had decided to go with Joyce Ma and Barbara McKibbin, who were off to spend the afternoon and night in Kyoto. "Last time, I spent three whole days there, staying in a temple. I took a bottle of Scotch with me, and that was a big hit. Those Buddhist monks are so cute. They love to drink and they love to flirt." Tall bamboos rustled outside the glass walls of the bathhouse. Mist-filled morning sunlight filtered through in slanting rays that danced in sequinned pinpoints when the bathers' cupped hands or bent knees were lifted to shatter the bright water. "We really must bring Denis here," Mary Russell said, referring to the *Vogue* photographer Denis Piel.

JOYCE Ma was busily engaged in marking or erasing numbers on her Issey Miyake order forms—a booklet with page after page of line drawings of that season's tops and bottoms in rows, like drying laundry. Barbara McKibbin was poring over a notebook containing her record of expenses. The train was moving fast, through countryside where bent-backed figures cultivated postage stamp–size fields, and futons hung airing in the sunshine on balconies or blue tiled roofs. I saw someone in a straw hat climb a ladder into a laden orange tree, and a saffron-robed figure with a bamboo fishing pole sitting next to a pond.

Joyce Ma glanced flickeringly at the scene, then reached up with an impatient gesture to adjust a metal ornament that nestled round her neck. It might have been a Balinese antiquity of forgotten religious significance. "There is so much pressure in this business," she said. "I was the first in Hong Kong to have the French and the Italians. But it's always the same, in the end. Valentino, Soprani, Basile—I lost the exclusive on them all. Now I go in more for the directional—the Japanese."

In the distance was a familiar-looking snow-capped cone. In the foreground, a group was coming across a dirt track through the fields, in black robes that flapped and flew out in the wind from the passage of the high-speed train. I asked my companions why they thought Japanese fashion was creating such a stir.

"It looks *new*," Barbara McKibbin said.

"Paris and Milan *died* a long time ago," Joyce Ma said.

"I feel a closeness between Japanese business people and American business people," Barbara McKibbin said. "There's a sense of efficiency. They're on our wavelength."

"Wanamaker is doing a Japanese festival."

"So is Bloomingdale's."

The mountain was almost on top of us. "Surely that's Mount Fuji?" I ventured.

Joyce Ma has in the course of many visits developed a pidgin Japanese, and she launched it firmly in the direction of a man drowsing over his newspaper on the far side of the aisle. "Fuji-san?" she asked, pointing.

The man's wife leaned forward from the window seat, a half-peeled orange in her hands, her expression as startled as his. At length, he conceded Fuji's identity. *"Gaijin,"* he murmured, shaking his newspaper rustlingly back into reading position.


In Tokyo again, I met up with Barbara and Selma Weiser at the From 1st Building, which houses, among other things, a Miyake boutique and showroom and a French restaurant called Le Poisson Rouge. In the restaurant, the two women were sitting at a table in a little room-within-a-room.

Selma Weiser, beneath a rather free interpretation of a Picasso, ordered a bottle of Chablis. She looked thoroughly revitalized since I had seen her in New York. "This is *fun*," she said. "We're having a great time in Tokyo."

With some linguistic difficulty, we ordered lunch.

"Want to know how I got into this line of work?" Selma Weiser asked, with an expansive wave of her glass.

"Mother!" Barbara Weiser said.

"When I was seven years old, I always remember," Selma Weiser went on, "I was at the old Pennsylvania Station, with *my* mother, and all these people were running around with suitcases heading for what seemed like swell places. And I said 'Who *are* all these people?' and she said 'They're *buyers*, child,' and that was it, for me. Of course, my very first trip as a buyer I went all the way to Ventnor, New Jersey."

Barbara Weiser said that people were so courteous here, so hospitable.

"We've done business for ten or twelve years with some people in Italy, in France," said her mother. "Not one of them has ever offered us so much as a cup of coffee."


AT THE store called Parco, passionately fashionable youths and girls in New Wave clothes and with foot-high spikes of blue-black hair, like cocks' combs, either shopped for the latest or sold it. Salespeople greeted browsers with a sketch of an obeisance, a slurred, James Dean–ish version of old courteous phrases of welcome. Selma Weiser paused before one boutique—gray-painted cement floor and walls framing sparse racks hung with what looked at first like clusters of large black bats. "Comme des

Garçons—Rei Kawakubo's line," she said, with an excited little nod, then plunged in to pull out first one hanger, then another, shaking the strange-looking garments into dancing life. "Isn't it great?" she said of a ragged-looking sweater with only one sleeve.

Beside us, a young woman stood gazing with intense solemnity at her reflection in a full-length glass. She wore a squashed black Comme des Garçons hat, which, though apparently new, looked at the same time immemorially old, like something that used to be a hat long ago. I expected its crown to pop open like a tuna-fish can, revealing a nest of birds in the young woman's hair. She went on standing there, her black eyes fixed on the reflection of her shoes—huge, monstrous, coal-black ski-boot things, with dangling white price tags.

One after another, Selma Weiser wiggled garments with what looked like moth holes in them. She put the tip of one finger into a little slit from the inside; it showed through pink against the black. "It's crazy, but we love it," she said.

"It's so comfortable," said Barbara Weiser. "It's like wearing soft old underwear—torn underwear."

We were all three giggling, then guffawing, out of something like affection. The young saleswomen looked on with sweet but unsmiling faces. The young customer was still looking gravely down at her boots.

"Know what?" Selma Weiser said. "When I get back home, I'm taking last year's leftover stock and cutting *holes* in it."

I asked how she was able to respond with enthusiasm to new fashions year after year.

She wiped away the tears of mirth. "I always hit the market as though I were a clothes-crazy size-five twenty-year-old," she said, looking almost serious.


·    ·    ·

"NINETEEN-SIXTY-NINE! The great moment in New York! *Dionysus! Hair!* Every day, I was so *excited.* I saw then what it could be—modern life." Issey Miyake, whose first name means "one life," who limps when he is tired, and whose mother perished at Hiroshima, sometimes wears a jaunty mustache and sometimes doesn't. He wore one when he was advertising whiskey on TV. (Like the film director Akira Kurosawa, he appeared as a "Suntory Personality.") On this drizzling evening, in the working-class Tokyo district of Asakusa, Miyake was clean-shaven and so passed relatively unnoticed by his fellow-citizens pushing in sidewalk battalions toward a festival in a Shinto shrine. The heads of many of those who jostled in the damp and lamplit air sported on the brows traditional rolled-up cotton bandannas tied in rabbit-ear knots. Miyake, who was wearing characteristic pants of somewhat baggy cut and one of a wardrobe of exquisitely unmilitary battle jackets of his own design, has dark, wavy hair, a puckish face, and a brown complexion, which sometimes led strangers to think him North African when he lived in Paris. (Between 1966 and 1969, he worked for the couturiers Guy Laroche and Givenchy.) His gestures, too, are Mediterranean. When he gets really enthusiastic, his eyes look heavenward, his forehead wrinkles, and his agile hands shape themselves as if to unscrew jelly jars, then start circling each side of his head in ever-widening whizzings and whirrings. His grip on a borrowed umbrella took up one hand at this moment, limiting him to wheels around a single ear. "Every night, parties! I was so influenced by Janis Joplin, Jimi Hendrix. But I did too much. I was too tired, got sick, came back to Japan."

Inch by inch, the crowd around was pushing purposefully on. People carried gaudily ornamented bamboo leaf rakes—symbols of the old commercial year, which they would discard at the temple entrance and exchange for newer, larger models.

"I began to think I could work here," said Miyake. "There was a new movement, a kind of underground, and I found it. In Paris, they said, 'Do Japanese,' and I said, 'No, no, I can't.' Then I said to myself, 'But *why* can't I? I'm *Japanese*!' I saw that all design must start with the fabric. I wanted to do something like blue jeans, and I had the idea to use the *sashiko* quilted cotton, like the cloth peasants wear." He gave a wave that took in a woman walking nearby who was dressed in humble traditional stuffs. "It is from workers, countrywomen bringing things in to market, that I learned to love Japanese women," he said grandly. "I like very much to use real people to show my clothes," he went on. "On the boat in New York, the Choral Society was office workers, teachers, a doctor who had to leave because a woman was having a baby." Miyake's fashion shows ("Fly with Issey Miyake," for example, and "Issey Miyake and Twelve Black Girls," both designed with Eiko Ishioka) have been legendary spectacles—an evanescent performance oeuvre. "Models are a dead thing for me now, a little bit," he said, skipping off the curb to execute a quick, dismissive parody of the runway mannequin's twist of hip, wrist, and shoulder. On the cover of *East Meets West,* a book by Miyake that was published some years back, Iman Haywood's red-sashed narrow waist and small brown Burmese-cat face float out incorporeally from an ink-dark ground. Some of the most compelling images on the inside pages, though, are not of models but of Miyake's Japanese contemporaries and friends (and also a diminutive, bespectacled woman member of the Japanese Diet, who was eighty at the time) wearing Issey Miyake clothes.

The crowd was approaching the temple precincts now, catching dazzling glimpses of a forecourt that was like a festive, brilliant-colored cave. Feet and pulses pounded. Serious elbowing set in. With the force of a mighty waterfall meeting a pool, the crowd debouched into the already teeming tentlike canvas cavern of the temple forecourt and was absorbed in a winking, clashing mass of color. Walls and stalls were papered, stacked, packed with new rakes for sale—as small as backscratchers or as large as trees, and ornamented with a profusion of greenery, coins, blossoms, fruits, bags of rice, puffy-cheeked doll masks, twists of rope, birds. Miyake was swept along with head back, mouth ajar, eyes bright and racing over the scene. "Brings good luck to merchants," he said. "Very Kansai, no?" he added, with a grin, referring to Kansai Yamamoto, a fellow-designer, known professionally as Kansai, who draws heavily on the emblems of Japanese folk art. The advancing hordes launched coins through the air toward the shrine itself, where priests sat on a platform smoking and being served food and sake by kimonoed women—all of them behind the safety of a net, as if they were picnicking inside a hockey goal. The general hullabaloo was punctuated often by banzailike chants and rhythmic clappings as teams of stallholders dispatched purchasers and rakes with benedictions. The crowd swirled and eddied. In the backwater behind one stall, a young girl looked up from a fan magazine with a young samurai movie star on the cover and caught sight of Miyake. "Ah, Kenzo-san," she said, with an intake of breath, then retreated behind her magazine in shame when she realized she had named another of Miyake's fellow-designers by mistake. At another stall, a squared-faced young man with a bad complexion was standing and chatting easily with the proprietor. Miyake greeted him. He was Kankuro, the Kabuki star.

ON THE following morning, a little red train rattled through the country-side beyond Tokyo. (No *shinkansen* this but a string of homely carriages, like rectangular links of sausage.) Issey Miyake sat with the latest issue of French *Vogue* on his knee and flipped through a special section on Japanese fashion. He came to a picture of women in pastel silk kimonos standing in front of a painted screen, and let the heavy pages fall shut, releasing a puff of expensive-paper smell. "Always they go back with the image of 'Old Japan,' " he said, giving the cover an exasperated tap. "I try always to show what is *modern* Japan."

Makiko Minagawa was sitting across the aisle. Her hair was tied up on top of her head in a perky sprout, like the neatly bound tufts of rice straw lined up in the tiny fields outside the windows. Beyond her sat one of Miyake's design assistants—a tall, gangling young man wearing a cowl-draped shawl and a solemn expression that was fitting in a subordinate whom Miyake had in a single breath reprimanded for having almost missed the train and credited with the creation of the recycled-egg-carton hat I had seen modelled on the U.S.S. *Intrepid.*

"I never look at fashion magazines when I am preparing a collection," Miyake said. "I prefer to see *National Geographic, Geo.* There was a man called Fujiwara who did a series of photographic essays about India and Tibet which was like a Bible to me. I'm very much influenced by Rauschenberg and Christo as artists—how they think of things excites me. And Leni Riefenstahl's *Nuba*—do you know it? That book influenced me so much. Here were naked people, but how creative they could be with their bodies and expressions! For me, the body is the most important part of fashion. What I learned in Paris is how the body is beautiful. In Japanese culture, the kimono conceals, transforms the body in a spiritual and philosophical way, makes a package."

On the horizon, a rosy frieze of pointed mountains seemed to shift with the progress of the train. Miyake leaned toward the window in excitement over the more immediate sight of some huge white radishes hung to dry on lines under pine trees and looking like little laundered long johns billowing in a wind. "For a long time, Japanese businessmen could not believe that anything creative could happen in Japan," he went on, leaning back in his seat. "There was never publicity for young Japanese designers—always for foreign names. They say always that my clothes just hang, like potato sacks—all right for foreign women but not for Japanese. But things are changing now. It is difficult for European designers at the moment. They are proud, they have all that wonderful tradition. Paris fashion has a wonderful history. I thought once it was impossible to do fashion without that background. But then I came to realize that everyone has a tradition. Japan, India—everybody. I'm not a traditional designer, like a designer in Paris. But that means I'm *free.*"

JUNICHI Arai, whose fabric-weaving studio was our journey's destination, wore a black smock and love beads, and had shoulder-length hair. His poetic, idealistic style was probably appropriate for a man pursuing his contemporary craft in a province that used to be (in the heyday of those pastel kimonos and obis) a thriving center of the textile-weaving industry but whose economy is now as eroded as the leaves chewed on by the remaining silkworms. Arai sat at the head of a large table, which was soon covered with tossed, unfurled, and tumbled sample lengths from his looms. Miyake's group and Arai's were all dressed in neutral colors, and the fabrics on the table were neutral, too. The only vivid touches in the room were orange emblems on the cover of a book on Tantric art, scarlet handles of a pair of shears, and hot-pink espadrilles worn as house shoes by one of Arai's young assistants. Miyake plucked at the samples, stroked them, smelled them, gathered them up in his fist; he tossed one piece over his shoulder like a toga, stuck another on his head like a hat; he did his rolling-up-of-invisible-sleeves gestures, his sketches of imaginary sheaths for arms and legs; he joked; he seemed to fall in love with the reverse of a fabric, then with a length of Tibetan wood bark that had served as a shipping tube; he stood up suddenly to bow politely as an ancient kimonoed woman passed shuffling through the room, and she paused to bow low to Miyake in return. An enormous black digital watch on Arai's wrist pinged away the afternoon in quarter hours. The egg-carton hatter looked more solemn than ever as he held fabrics right up to his nose, apparently counting the threads. "I want to splash Jackson Pollock colors on," Miyake said, turning to me and speaking in English. "Only black and neutral makes too somber, too straight." Arai, who had left the room, now came back with a roll of black-and-gray stuff in his arms and a mischievous look in his eye. Miyake looked, stroked, joked again. But his face was shadowed by resentment, just the same: the fabric had been commissioned by Rei Kawakubo, the designer of Comme des Garçons.

PERHAPS French *Vogue*'s photographer never drove through the dingy little towns of Gumma Prefecture on a late-November afternoon. Under a sullen, sulfurous sky crisscrossed by overhead power lines stretched main streets of cement-block stores filled with gimcrack dinette furniture and children's tricycles, and buttressed by sidewalk piles of plastic beverage cases—red for Coca-Cola, yellow for Kirin beer. Here was a shabby-looking public bathhouse, there a McDonald's. Here was a pink awning reading "Porno Shop," and a peeling poster of a bare-breasted Western woman in a provocative pose; there, as if signifying upward yearning, was a Hanae Mori boutique. In a vacant lot near a rusting auto hulk stood a single, dusty ginkgo tree.

Inside the car, Miyake, Arai, and Makiko Minagawa were discussing Japanese creativity. It was reluctantly agreed that Italy was a creative nation and Japan was not.

"Kyoto is creative, though," Miyake said. "Makiko is from Kyoto." He said that her grandfather had brought about a great renaissance in hand-painting kimonos in Kyoto. "Very civilized, very cultured people there." There was a slight pause. "I am from Hiroshima," he said. "Hiroshima has no culture." He laughed. "Famous only for its oysters."

There was another slight pause. "For its oysters. And for the atomic bomb."

"THIS region is famous for mushrooms, wind off mountains, strength of its women," Makiko Minagawa said to me as we sat side by side on a railway-station bench waiting for the Tokyo train. Apart from us, the egg-carton hatter, and Miyake, who stood with his back to us a little way off, puffing on a cigarette, there were only, on the length of the windswept, dark platform, three separate wedding parties. The farthest group looked almost prosperous, with guests in kimonos or silver four-in-hands carrying bulging packages of wedding-feast favors. The nearest group, raucous with *sake* laughs, was cheaply dressed, and put down lean-looking shopping bags to toss high in the air first the wiry little bridegroom and then (after waggish consultations) his sturdy, far larger-looking bride as well. The train arrived—a broad and blurred red band sketched quickly in as background to the sharply focussed, solitary black-clad figure of Miyake. There was a popping of firecrackers and rocketlike streamers; the three couples each wheeling a single colored fiber-glass suitcase of identical style, boarded the train. Miyake slid down into his seat, muttering, "I can't stand weddings." As the train slid past the three groups of wedding guests left behind on the platform, they let out ritual chants of farewell. Three faint chorussed shouts sounded in syncopation; three sets of parallel upraised arms, flushed faces, mouths in a wide O slipped by as the train gathered speed. The carriage was noisy, steamy, filled with the sounds of grownups singing and of children being tickled. Miyake dropped his head to his chest and fell asleep.

· · ·

ARATA Isozaki, the architect (I first saw him on page 28 of *East Meets West*: pale linen suit, ironic expression), was at home that evening to a group of visiting French architects. Some of these sat at Isozaki's long white drafting table, opposite specially hired sushi workers deftly rolling balls of cooked rice in the palms of their hands. Other Frenchmen, wilting from jet lag, culture shock, and Folonari Soave, sat dozily nodding over folded arms in a darkened room adjacent, where a slide show flickered along. A group of Japanese architects sat in the foyer eating cannelloni. Some of the Frenchmen were accompanied by their wives, who clustered round Miyake with excited Parisian cries. Our hostess was the only Japanese woman present—a small, imperious figure dressed like a gaucho general, in a black Miyake jodhpur-jumpsuit and Third World jewelry.

*"Madame Isozaki est sculpteur,"* Miyake said in introducing her.

A Frenchman with a hussar's mustachios and very florid shirt stripes stood handing out copies of a book about himself. "They told us to bring gifts to Japan," he said. "I'm not embarrassed about this, because I didn't write it."

"I think you would find that all the younger architects in the room would describe themselves as between postmodern and New Wave," said Arata Isozaki, and he opened a book to demonstrate the difference between his style and that of the American architect Michael Graves. "I call this my Marilyn Monroe chair," he said, showing me a photograph.

Miyake was looking at a poster pinned on the wall. Inside a cosmic bubble were seas, fires, gods, and cross-legged Buddhas, all painted in red, blue, green, and gold; below the bubble reared a rampant turtle in the embrace of a snake. "Look," Miyake said. "The Mandala show in the museum at the department store La Forêt."

.   .   .

FLORID-STRIPES pulled up in a taxi at the Hotel Okura just as I was picking up my room key. *"Est-ce que Madame Rykiel est arrivée?"* he demanded of the startled and uncomprehending night clerk. *"Madame Sonia Rykiel!"* the man repeated, louder. *"Est-elle dans l'hôtel?"*

I LAY down in the dark. Beside my head, in a small blue glow, an electronic clock repeatedly gave birth to digits and instantly obliterated them. My own jet lag had taken unshakable hold. Sleep as I once knew it was gone—a piece of cozy, familiar luggage left behind in a land on the other side of the wardrobe and far, far away. I lay for years or minutes in a whirl of hallucinatory fragments where people with unfamiliar faces speaking meaningless words bowed and boarded endless trains. I sat bolt upright, read a page of my hotel-bookstore paperback about the Japanese Mind, lay down again. Some unseen hand in the hallway slid a folded copy of the *Japan Times* into the crack of yellow light under my door. I opened the curtains. On the roof of the Nippon Mining Company building, opposite, a red-and-white national flag hung limp against a blood-red dawn. I opened the newspaper and read about a police-corruption scandal in Osaka Prefecture; two high-ranking officers had already committed suicide. Inside a cagelike structure on the roof, a single athletic figure appeared, ran round and round and round, then of a sudden sprang upside down on its hands. A fat brown bird on my windowsill tweeted and dipped up and down, as if out of gymnastic solidarity.

"BARBARA and I are having a *great* time. Aren't we, Bobbie?" Selma Weiser said as she put down her bulging handbag and sat down to breakfast. She keeps four fat address books: one for the States, one for France, one for Italy, and one for "miscellaneous countries," including

England, India, and Japan. "Tell about your interview with Yohji, Bobbie. Go ahead."

In spite of the Weisers' long-standing connections with Miyake, Kansai, and Kenzo, and their appreciation of Rei Kawakubo, it is the designer Yohji Yamamoto who wears Charivari's particular colors in the great competitive horse race of Japanese fashions. For several years, Selma Weiser's stores had "the exclusive" on Yamamoto. "We made a big Yohji statement" was how she put it. Now Barbara Weiser was preparing a presentation on Japanese fashion for The Fashion Group in New York—an organization of people involved in all aspects of the apparel and cosmetics industries. She had taped an interview with Yamamoto.

"I asked him how he saw his customer—you know, the standard question," Barbara Weiser said. "Know what he said? 'A person not quite young. Who gets slim. Not quite man, not quite woman. In the rain, with the wind blowing in her face.' No, wait for it, I'm not kidding: 'In the rain. With the wind blowing in her face. And *smoking a cigar!*' "

Selma Weiser was rocking with laughter; her eyes, under the cosmetically shadowed lids, were overflowing with tears. "Don't you *love* it?" she asked. " 'Not quite woman . . . A cigar!' Can't you just see The Fashion Group reacting to *that*? The only thing those people want to know is 'Is the customer for this line Junior or Contemporary?' "


IN THE silent grounds of the Imperial Palace, crows strutted by the massive donjon walls. In the Eastern Gardens, people sat looking up, then down again to their watercolor pads. Huge red-white-and-blue carp, like underwater fighting kites, blipped in ponds and passed through the shade under ornamental footbridges. The sun was warm. In the far distance, at the end of the wide gravelled drive, uncountable people-specks climbed out of buses to stand shoulder to shoulder for photographers. At my elbow, a Western woman dressed all in black, her tourist map slowly unfolding itself on her crossed knee, sat calmly smoking a cigarette. She smiled. Her face was long, sunburned, as gentle as the muzzle of a Dutch rabbit or of certain breeds of sheep. She was breaking her journey from New Zealand to England, and was on the point of being ordained a Methodist minister.

"I MET my friend Hino first on the plane from New York, then again one day when I was having lunch with Stevie Wonder," Issey Miyake said in the car that evening. He sat sidewise in the front passenger seat with his elbow crooked and his brown hand resting on the white lace antimacassar. We were passing through avenues of Tokyo neon; patches and flashes of color entered the car and flew seamlessly over our faces like a wind. Harumi Fujimoto (she's on page 30 of *East Meets West: sashiko* knit) sat in the back seat with me. She had a broad, flat, lively face and a thick, helmetlike mop of hair dipping crisply into a central nosepiece effect. "Everyone calls me Pickle," she had said.

Miyake had found some clothes of his design for Hino to wear onstage for his jazz-rock concert. "Many people ask me," he said. "Grace Jones, Mick Jagger, Miles Davis, Diana Ross. Last year, I did costumes for Maurice Béjart. When I saw his *Romeo and Juliet* in 1968, I thought 'This man is a god.' Alvin Ailey asked me, but it was my collection time in Paris." The hand lifted itself off the lace and began to wave as he talked about stage performances, then about the New Kabuki director Ennosuke, who created *Nambuki Love Story*. "So dramatic, the staging; such beautiful kimono; two hundred actors on stage. It's incredible!" His hand had been steadily winding itself to fire off his highest praise: "It's so *free*!"

. . .

SOME ten thousand young people had arrived promptly at six-thirty for Hino's concert, settling into the giant arena as gently as snow. The jazz-rock star was a slim, almost fragile-looking young man with a small face, which puffed out as he played his trumpet. ("Like a blowfish" was how Miyake described Hino's cheeks at full toot.) Wearing black leather pants, a samurai dagger, and a particolored wing-shoulder wet-suit-fabric jacket, Hino was holding his own against an elaborate backup band and a set with energetic lighting in which the words "Damon," "Pyramid," and "Hino" blinked, coursed, and pulsed in a ceaseless show of vivid color. "He was also a Suntory Personality," Miyake said to me, whispering, as though we were sitting at a string-quartet recital. Around us, indeed, were very few weaving heads or tapping feet; the audience seemed almost eerily calm. The lit-up words clashed brightly on in a swirl of colored-smoke effects, like Hades. In shafts of purple air, the band turned blue, Hino red, and the teetering brass cymbals magenta.

A man with dark aviator glasses and a gravelly voice came out onstage and told some jokes. A man with a wispy mustache and a triangle of beard joined him. He wore a fashionable mechanic's-coverall jumpsuit with a yellow muffler as an R.A.F.–style ascot. He took a rolled-bandanna headband out of a pocket and put it on, then led the finally almost lively audience in what appeared to be ritualistic football cheerleaders' chants, with rhythmic handclaps and mysterious yells. His arms were going up and down like semaphore flags.

"Who is this man?" I asked.

"Very powerful art director," said Miyake, turning to me a face still lit with happy laughter. "Very famous graphic designer. Amateur table-tennis champion."

. . .

A KNOT of people hung around the door of Hino's dressing room, and there was a fragrant smell from bouquets of red-and-white flowers inside.

"Ah, Kankuro-san!" said Miyake to the Kabuki actor, who was on his way out.

*"Dozo, dozo,"* Hino said, beckoning Miyake in.

The musician had changed into a pink version of the coverall jumpsuit (Miyake's design) and was giving autographs. Very young girls were waiting, shyly giggling behind their hands, then presenting him with record sleeves to sign, or with flowers. They stood in a line and bowed and bowed, and he bowed back as he took a program and a felt pen and, with a tremendous flourish, wrote, in English, "Love! Hino."

The printed program was very splendid, and had a lot of photographs. In one, Hino's slender, jockeylike form was seen in a whirlpool tub, where he sat gazing pensively into the frothing waters within arm's reach of a bottle of some manly fragrance made by Damon. ("Very big cosmetic company," said Miyake.) In another, Hino sat fully clad, respectfully playing his trumpet for a grizzle-haired American jazz teacher in the Master's messy and far from luxurious living room in New York on what looked like a very hot summer's day.

THE Italian restaurant was empty and exquisite; it had been kept open as a particular service to our party at this late hour of ten o'clock. The lighting in the room was careful and velvet, modulating here and there in pools of ambiguity. On a sideboard, a many-armed candelabra and a sheaf of pale-green celery in an ornate silver wine cooler seemed to hover at the center of a gauzy shimmer. The cheerleader had come along to supper. His name was Katsumi Asaba, and he crouches rather menacingly on page 31 of *East Meets West* in a pair of Ultrasuede pants. He was accompanied this evening by his young wife, who looked like Hedy Lamarr. He had a nervous way of giving little nods as he talked or made Japanese listening-and-agreeing sounds, as if he were shaking a raindrop from the end of his nose. Miyake said that Asaba had a fantastic team working with him, a particularly brilliant and famous copywriter. Asaba was the creator of the new advertising campaign called Tasteful Life, which was built around Woody Allen. The campaign was for Seibu, the giant department-store company and conglomerate. Seibu's museum of art had held a great show of Picasso's work in Tokyo. "The department stores are the keepers of the culture here at the moment," Miyake said.

THE thread between the Hotel Okura and Mme. Mori's butterfly-shaped headquarters began to tighten as the week wore on. Each morning, a new batch of tissue-nestled orchid plants with Mme. Mori's card was carried up from the hotel florist in the lobby to the rooms of fresh arrivals from the international fashion world. "M. Valentino Garavani," read one card. "Miss Norma Kamali," "Mme. Sonia Rykiel," and "Mme. Hebe Dorsey," read others. An upward movement of orchids also signified the presence in town of the New York interior designer and display director Robert Currie, who was to work on the staging of the "Best Five" fashion shows and effect one of his four-times-yearly changes of the Hanae Mori Building's windows, which on the occasion of my luncheon with their owner had been artistically draped with lengths of fat seagoing rope. The complex, rhythmic life of the Okura lobby went on as usual. Brown-uniformed bellboys darted this way and that with messages and tinkling bells. Kimonoed maidens performed their duty of bowing guests in and out of elevators. On one wall, a star-spangled map of the world continued listing, before curious and incurious passersby alike, the time at that particular instant in Abu Dhabi, Phoenix, Bangkok, Baghdad. (The present in New York always seemed to be on some other day entirely.) In sharp outline against the soothing suffused light from the paper-screen back wall, businessmen sat reading the *Asian Wall Street Journal* in spiky-legged chairs shaped like upturned limpets. Across the lobby, other businessmen passed in and out of the entrance doors—twin parallel membranes of automatically sliding glass, like an elongated video screen, framing an outside world crisply lit by sunshine tinged with the green of leaves. At the curb, remote-controlled doors of taxicabs popped open and shut like flippers as white-gloved commissionaires surrendered guests to the charge of white-gloved drivers.

Valentino, the Italian designer, close-sheathed in his double-breasted suit, crossed the lobby and headed for his waiting car. With a Napoleonic flat-palm touch to his jacket buttons and some slight rear-rangement of his facial expression, he seemed to be accepting as his due the deferential, whispered parting of the electronic doors. Then he was gone, and other shapes filled the screen. A woman dressed like a Japanese peasant—Sonia Rykiel's daughter and manager, Nathalie—consulted in French with a woman dressed like a Peruvian peasant and with Sonia Rykiel. The French designer was in her habitual Bunraku puppeteer's black tunic silhouette, with thin black-stockinged legs, and slightly turned-out feet in Chinese cotton Mary Janes. The effect was completed by two large artificial chrysanthemums pinned on one hip; two flat purses nestling, one attached to the other, like Siamese twins, on the other hip; and a fluff of ginger-gold hair. The group went off to The Space to address itself to the question of selecting models for the Sonia Rykiel fashion show. The buying team from the Browns fashion shops in London con-cluded the business part of its trip and went off to Atami to soak at the hot springs. Selma and Barbara Weiser decided to extend their trip. Their mother-and-daughter silhouettes, in closely similar outfits combining feeling for Yohji Yamamoto and feeling for Kawakubo, and with handbags full of order books and agendas, came and went busily through the doors of the Okura as they tested the waters of commerce at apparel companies with names like Obscure Desire and Brains. They went off to Kyoto. They bought so much at Mr. Nishimura's old-kimono shop that they had to buy another suitcase, too. They came back. They went to a Japanese inn for a traditional meal.

"There was this one dish I didn't care for, somehow," Selma Weiser said. "Little ground-up things." She measured off a length along her thumb and looked at it with distaste. "I'll give you three guesses what they were."

I gave up.

Her laugh came rolling in, crested in outraged delight. "It was *bees*!"


THE artistic ropes had gone from the Hanae Mori Building, and two artistically parked, bunting-draped new Nissan automobiles sat outside nosing at the freshly arranged fashion windows. Upstairs in The Space, Norma Kamali and Sonia Rykiel (wired, like their audience, to earplugs for simultaneous translations into and out of English, French, and Japanese) sat publicly discussing the topic "Does fashion create an age, or does the age create fashion?" An audience of solemn, gray-suited men sat straight-spined, with fists on knees (except when they made an occasional note with one of the ballpoints that Nissan had provided with the programs), on the surrounding bleacherlike seating. The panel's moderator, a man with Latin-style tinted spectacles and an air of world-weariness, sat between the two women, whom he addressed as Kamali-san and Rykiel-san. He was from the newspaper *Asahi Shimbun,* whose interests seemed to be allied with Mme. Mori's own. A third member of the panel was an

*Asahi Shimbun* fashion reporter; a fourth was a fashion reporter for *The New York Times.*

"It is creative people who make the times!" said Rykiel-san. The words came bursting out of her slight, black-clad person with tremendous force. She had a narrow, triangular face—dead-white, deeply lined, and framed by her fuzzy cloud of ginger hair, which had the shape of a pyramid and the texture of cotton candy. Her eyes darted, feverishly bright, under bangs that almost hid them. "There is no such thing as national or international fashion, as couture or prêt-à-porter," she said, with feeling. "Only more or less worthwhile artists. Receiving. Transmitting. Creatures apart."

Norma Kamali said she got a lot of her inspiration from what people wore on the streets. As she sat behind her name transmuted into red-painted Japanese script, at a white-shrouded table in a white-painted space, Kamali-san's appearance was not to be outdone by Mme. Rykiel's. Norma Kamali's lips and nails were glossy red, and a rosy highlight of rouge curled up each cheekbone and around the outer eye like a question mark. Twinkling metal minnows dangled from her earlobes. She had dressed her long, dark hair in center-parted puffs that rose like horns, casting a blue-shadow visor on her brow and echoing larger, yeasty curves on the shoulders of her Kamali suit. "From now on, I want to come often to Japan," she said. "I want to get my hands on the fabric of the future."

The gray-suited men looked on and listened impassively.

"If we in the industry aren't careful, people will say, 'Fashion—who needs it?'" said the American fashion reporter, who had only just arrived in Tokyo, where the question isn't very often posed.

"Japan had the kimono and a very old tradition. It is not a new country, like the United States," said the Japanese fashion reporter with a certain firmness.

I imagined the voices merging and melting into the single, tiny

French-speaking voice insinuated into Sonia Rykiel's ear. She puckered her mouth with an impatient look. She lifted a pale hand and played with her pale lip. She slid her fingers under the half-moon lace-bib neckline of her black Rykiel sweater and rubbed her collarbone gently, as if for comfort.

The moderator said that as women began to gain equality with men they would have to dress more sexily in order to attract them.

Abruptly, Sonia Rykiel left off twining a strand of hair around her finger. "Attracting men is not what women want to do," she said. " 'Sexy' does not mean clothes. That's why I called my autobiography *I Would Prefer Her Naked.*" The gray suits went on listening, as still as could be. "Men are more sexy without clothes, after all," Rykiel-san said. The gray suits shifted, with an almost imperceptible rustle.

AT THE Isetan department store, a long feather in the elevator girl's bowler hat trembled as she warblingly described the riches to be found on each successive floor. I got out at random. The floor stretched to its farthest reaches with familiar names and goods: J. Press, J. G. Hook, Brooks Brothers, Perry Ellis, Norma Kamali, Calvin Klein. (Japanese companies pay large sums—it is said that Isetan pays a million dollars a year to Klein —for the right to manufacture designs under license, resized for smaller, Japanese figures.) A plaster mannequin with Western features and dressed in a Ralph Lauren–style frontierswoman blouse stood with its arm bent back at an unnatural angle from its elbow joint. It stared out from under swooping, wirelike black lashes at a nearby poster in which a young, blond, American-looking model held a silver-colored gymnastic weight in her upraised fist. "HEALTHY," the poster read. On the floor above, old-style, floor-living Japanese furniture—armrests, low tables, dressing tables to kneel before—looked somehow shamefaced, as if it were being squeezed and flattened by the huge, inflated-looking Conran's-style sofas that stood next to it. Up again, to a department active with the busy tick, the flashing pendulum of a thousand clocks, and to a kimono department, where finely tuned discussions about pale silk yard goods and obi lengths proceeded to a crooning overlay of Peggy Lee. Then, on the floor above—where people were milling at the entrance to the store's museum and its Toulouse-Lautrec show—I turned a corner to mount an empty flight of stairs and heard the noisy twittering of birds. The bird-department salesman looked up as I passed. Dozens of his small charges sat on his arms, his shoulders, his fingers, and the top of his head as he fed them seed from a cardboard shoebox. I opened a door and came onto a roof with Astro Turf, a distant carousel, a man lying sleeping on a bench in the bright sun. A bonsai department had a one-foot tree bearing fourteen full-size pears. Large blue plastic tanks like swimming pools held segregated masses of small, larger, largest lobsters. Other tanks contained hierarchic, circling schools of red-white-and-blue-patterned fish. From the far side of the roof garden appeared a worker wearing baggy blue cotton pants (not unlike some of Issey Miyake's menswear designs) and trundling a wheelbarrow filled with frilly pink-and-white cabbages, which he proceeded with ferocious movements to plant cheek by jowl in fancy Italianate urns.

VALENTINO sat very upright on a bleacher seat in The Space, wearing huge dark glasses and a tiny muffler. The moment of my audience (arranged through Miss Suita, of Hanae Mori) had come up as a rehearsal was going on for the opening-night group fashion show of the "Best Five," when all the designers would offer compressed versions of shows they would present singly and at full length on one of the five subsequent days. First making some slight anticipatory adjustment of his features, Valentino

66

turned his face to me. He touched his white shirt cuffs, with their large gold links, as if signalling that I might now begin. "This is the most civilized country in the world!" he said, in his accented English. "The atmosphere! The people! The way they talk!" The lights over the empty bleachers suddenly dimmed as those on the runway brightened and the strains of "I Love Paris" started up. Valentino's face panned round to where a line of models in rainbow-colored Rykiel knits undulated across the brightly lit stage below and to his right. He brought his face back. His eyes were quite invisible. "Tokyo is so modern! So up to date!" he said. He snapped his fingers twice. His face strayed round again. The models were wearing turbans and Rykiel dresses in transparent lace fabric—white in front, black in back, with flesh-colored flesh in between. The face came sliding back. "Tokyo is a good runway," Valentino said.

Was he involved at all with the staging of his fashion shows?

"I just arrange the bow," he said. "Always my little touch!" As he leaned closer in the semidarkness, smiling and making a bow-arranging mime beneath his chin, I saw reflected from the convex surface of his sunglasses a strange hobgoblin who resembled me.

"O.K., which of you girls has the problem with changing?" a woman with yellow pants asked, in an Australian accent. (She was staging Mme. Mori's segment of the show.) Models with cheekbones and jawbones like blades and in dresses like whirligigs of ice cream—colored frills stood inspecting their fingernails. "O.K., everybody spin around! You! Stand still while the rest are spinning." *Pom-pom-de-pom* trilled the music. Valentino turned toward an interviewer from Japanese television, snapping off his glasses and his muffler as the camera lights came on. One of the models, a blonde, had her features completely blotted out with chalk-white foundation; even her eyelashes looked albino. "Fill up the whole stage! Keep twirling and twirling and looking pretty!" A tall black American model in a white pants suit was to tango with a Japanese model in a white dress. White Pants progressed across the apron runway with that models' step that is not exactly dancing, or walking, either: lifted knee, lower leg flipping out like a wooden leg, sole of the foot down, pause, then the heel. Yellow Pants stood in for the tango partner, even pretended to nibble on the black woman's neck.

In the lobby outside The Space, enormous, bosomy bouquets of white flowers, with ribbon sashes like those of beauty-pageant winners, stood on lines of pedestals. Kansai was waiting there to see his segment rehearsed. He wore combat boots and a denim vest with a rampant dragon embroidered on the back; from under a rolled-bandanna headband he smiled with large, square white teeth. A little girl of three or so stood staring at him, holding the string of a red balloon. For his recent "Passion Night" fashion show, admission, which included a commemorative T-shirt, had been eleven dollars. Eleven thousand people had attended. There had been thirty-eight models, fifty naked children, assorted rock stars, many motorbikes. "Fashion isn't everything," Kansai said. "So we make it entertainment. Sometimes we have fashion for entertainment. Sometimes golf." Sayoko, the world-famous Japanese model, was rehearsing in the lobby the traditional whirling-dervishlike Korean dance she was to perform as the climax of Kansai's show. She had done the same dance, in the same dress, for his earlier shows in Paris and New York. Her delicate, narrow, "Old Japan" face was tilted at an angle, with downcast eyes, as she turned in an embroidered cone of skirt and little scraps of pink silk slipper, beating on both ends of an egg timer–shaped drum that hung round her neck. "All of the earth is watching Japanese designers, now that we don't need it," Kansai said, barely glancing at Sayoko. "When our generation of designers started our own businesses, in the early seventies, the wind was all against us. Now people come, take back things—always for store windows, always for display. Press people come, write more and more crazy; it escalates. It's like a gold rush, a typhoon passing. Many people misunderstand." Sayoko twirled and twirled. The little girl was now watching her.

Nearby, Norma Kamali's woman assistant, dressed in a Kamali "rah-rah" miniskirt, was eating at full speed with chopsticks from a take-out cardboard lunchbox.

"So we got all the balloons?" Norma Kamali asked her.

"Eight hundred of them."

A model leaned against a wall chewing gum, a black hairnet over white bows of curlpaper. "Now all you have to do is figure out how to get them all in," she said.

The little silk slippers went on turning and turning, the muffled sound of the drum went on. By signs, I persuaded a Japanese man to accompany me to the lobby's bright-red public telephone. He listened politely to the unknown voice at the end of the wire, then drew a map (with fastidious featherings-in and erasures of street lines, delicate calligraphy) for me to give to a cabdriver.

The driver looked at the map from all angles, then grunted and roared off, delivering me to a sushi shop. The line of chefs behind the counter let out their yells of welcome as I stepped through the door. At the counter, Issey Miyake sat with a half-dozen other people. The conversation was all about models. It was generally agreed that when it came to the Texan model Jerry Hall you couldn't see the clothes at all, these days—you could see only Jerry Hall.


"I NEVER wear black tie," Miyake said on the way to the "Best Five" opening-night party, at L'Orangerie. "I would look ridiculous, like a waiter." His formal clothes consisted of a specially pleated battle tunic with an Arabian-style cowled shawl and bellows-shaped trousers, all in black. We made a stop en route at Seibu. There, in the store's entrance, was a huge poster with a mournful, childlike, inscrutable-looking Woody Allen gazing over the top of printed messages in Japanese, presumably referring to the Tasteful Life. Upstairs, the Seibu Museum of Art was holding an opening for a show of Memphis, the avant-garde Milanese design collective. Miyake's face lit up as he met the embrace of Ettore Sottsass, the Italian designer and a Memphis founding member. Sottsass was a bearlike man with a shaggy mustache and a rumpled, jet-lagged air. He was standing, his jacket unbuttoned, beside a display of his glassware designs—strange, luminous, blob-dotted pots and hand-blown amphorae in fairy-tale colors, like things dredged barnacled and glistening from the depths of some Mediterranean dream.

"Once, I went to a Chinese fortune-teller who read my palm," Miyake said as the car carried us across Tokyo to The Space. He seemed agitated in some way. "Japanese young people don't know how to find their lives," he said. "They think it is just given to them." He was silent for a time. "You must *fight* in life," he said, with sudden force.

As I left the elevator on the top floor of the Hanae Mori Building, I was in time to see Selma Weiser ascending on the escalator from the floor below, like a majestic ship's-figurehead in her ankle-length gown, with a tiny evening purse on her arm. Behind her rose Barbara Weiser, and then came Jon Weiser, freshly arrived that day, for the opening of the menswear-buying season. Ranks of small men in dinner jackets went into paroxysms of bowing as Miyake approached. He was whisked off to the head table in L'Orangerie, where he was seated next to Valentino.

With the arrival of some rubbery dessert pastries shaped like swans, two men seated opposite me and both wearing elaborately ruffled shirts ventured to try out their English.

"Have you heard of Japan Fashion Fair?" said one.

"I think kimono very, very good for Western woman," said the other. "Western woman very, very tall."

Each then grasped the lapel of his jacket and opened it with a magician's flourish to point to the label on the inside pocket.

The Space was filled with a buzz of guests. A little procession wound its way to seats in the front row: Norma Kamali, in flounced skirt and ear minnows (Japanese company under license, Renown); Sonia Rykiel, in her Bunraku black plus cheerleaders' red-and-white pom-poms at hip height (licensee, Seibu); Valentino, in formfitting dinner jacket (licensee, Mitsui); Kansai, in floatingly oversized white brocade bellhop jacket over baggy black Chico Marx pants; and Mme. Mori, in evening skirt and a jacket covered with sequinned butterflies. In front of me, an elderly Japanese woman turned to her neighbor with a little nod. "Those must be the designers," she said, in English. The president of the *Asahi Shimbun* made a speech. The governor of Tokyo made two speeches. "The world is now paying fervent attention to the Oriental delicacy and elegance of Japanese fashion," he said, in the speech he made in English, with his reading glasses on. Sonia Rykiel gazed around the room or played with her lip. Norma Kamali caught someone's eye and winked. Issey Miyake, a solitary all-black bird in a field of penguins, had found a seat in the highest and most distant row of bleachers and was looking thoughtful. John Fairchild, the publisher of *Women's Wear Daily* and *W*, left his seat, next to a woman in a spangle-sleeved white dress and elbow-length evening gloves. He was a prematurely white-haired man with a pink face and a receding chin. "We thank Her Gracious Imperial Majesty for coming within our presence to her very first fashion show," he said, aiming in the direction of the spangled sleeves a nervous flutter of quasi-Japanese obeisances. "To be really frank, there are only twenty-seven great fashion designers in the world," he said. Selma, Barbara, and Jon Weiser exchanged surreptitious, raised-eyebrow glances. Fairchild then introduced in turn the five of those Olympians at present sitting under his nose in the front row of The Space. "Hanae Mori is the em-press of international fashion," he said, rounding off his tributes.

As each chapter of the group fashion show started, each designer's image blossomed from a dozen video screens strategically scattered through the hall. *"Sono Valentino Garavani," "Je suis Sonia Rykiel,"* and "Hi, I'm Norma Kamali from New York City, U.S.A.," said the matched sets of images, from where they hovered over the heads of the audience or beamed up at it from the level of its knees. On the spot where the governor had spoken, models sinuously turned and posed. The elderly woman in front nodded approvingly at Valentino's segment—models with glittering Vs on their chests, casting sultry glances from under chamber-pot hats—and then looked infuriated at Kansai's segment when bare-chested men thrust forward martial-looking banners, and girls in hot-pink skirts had plastic rollers bristling in their hair. Sayoko did her dance. Then some magic-lantern clouds were puffily projected on the wall, and the Empire State Building (bent at an angle where wall met floor) came ethereally sliding in. Norma Kamali's new designs in denim, shirting, and thermal-underwear fabrics appeared on models and on "real people," too —strolling about, chewing gum, and holding on to large bunches of red balloons. One of the black models had travelled with her two-year-old daughter, who stole the scene in peaks of hair and diminutive dungarees. The ice cream–colored whirligigs came out, still twirling and twirling and looking pretty. The white pants suit tangoed. The black-and-white trans-parent-lace dresses served to jerk awake a man who had been sitting in the front row with his chin resting on his shirtfront. Then designers, models in rich fabrics and plunging necklines, and models in denim and T-shirts were all up on the stage together for a finale, holding on to red balloons and bouquets of flowers, swaying to the music of a song called "Big Bucks." The audience clapped in time, the princess's head was cheerily bouncing from side to side, the balloons were bobbing up and down. "Big bucks, big bucks, big bucks," ran the chorus, over and over.

People began gathering their pocketbooks and their complimentary copies of Japanese *W*; the princess held her gloves, which were like steamrollered silk arms. "Big bucks, big bucks . . . money is a universal language." The little moppet in dungarees was happily boogying to herself right at the front of the stage. Valentino, finding himself next to her, bent slightly toward her in his tuxedo. He held his hand at the height of his folded white linen breast-pocket handkerchief and curled and uncurled his fingers at her. *"Ciao,"* he said.

"WHAT was it all about, exactly?" Jon Weiser asked the next day.

Issey Miyake shrugged, smiled. "It is difficult to explain," he replied. "About how fragile is life, how things are not what they seem."

We were in a car, driving away from an afternoon performance of an avant-garde play. A man and a woman there had been, clearly; the rattle of rain on the window; a ramshackle door suddenly flung wide to shock us with the woman's swinging corpse; French pastries, in the intermission; the door flung wide again, this time on the hanging body of the man, and the woman somehow back in life. Autumn leaves had been onstage, for certain—hurled about, in drifts, or clinging to branches of a weeping willow and wildly waving in the mounting storm. And water! My, had there been water on that stage! It came swirling on in floods that forced the people in the first three rows of seats to duck hastily for cover behind specially provided plastic sheets. It came sloshing onstage in seas and phantasmal tides. It streamed from the black oilskins of men who came on carrying a fishing boat. It glued down the center-parted hair of the man—missionary or charlatan?—who came out of the storm in a sunflower-colored vest with a bicycle strapped to his back, then showed up again later (and yet wetter) to deliver himself of a tremendous oration as he stood perched high up on his bicycle saddle. And it dripped as mournfully as tears or blood from the broken, lifeless figure in a long white gown carried in her lover's arms—until, resurrected once more and in a small, prim hat, she sailed off with him into the evening sky.

"We must hurry, we are a little bit late," Miyake said. "We must be on time for the Mandala show at the museum of La Forêt."

ON THE department store's top floor, paying customers stood in a rapt semicircle while a pair of Bhutanese priests—one fat and one thin, and both in shoes with upturned, gnomish points—stood twirling prayer wheels and humming sacred hums. A priestly arm stretched out from time to time—a large gold watch ticked on the wrist below the yellow cuff of the purple sleeve—and opened one of many tiers of dollhouse-sized doors in an ornate gilt pagoda. This tiny temple turned; its beaded finial spun faster, then slower again; stillness came. The men stopped chanting and retired behind a curtain for a while to breathe in and out like mortal men. Jon Weiser, in a fashionable Italian leather jacket, went off to reconnoiter the fashion merchandise on the floors below. Miyake walked through the exhibition with Kazuko Koike, a woman with a sharply angled pompadour haircut and an avant-garde clothing style, who is an art director and an associate curator of the Seibu Museum. Illustrated notions of an ancient Asian cosmos—fire-breathing creatures, the turtle and the snake, multiarmed goddesses, Mt. Fuji—surrounded the pair as they discussed Miyake's international show, called "Bodyworks," in which he would present his ideas in unexpected media, such as rattan, plastic, or paper, on computerized pseudo human beings and on black silicone-fleshed forms. ("I want to forge ahead, to break the mold," he would say. "I want to find out what clothing might be.")

A stocky man dressed in a knee-length Tibetan robe tweaked aside a curtain and came out to join our group. He wore swinging sixties–style ankle boots below bare calves. His manner was jaunty and self-confident, and suggested that he was the closest thing two Bhutanese priests can have to a road manager. "Oh, no, I don't get into those protective deities, you see," he was saying, in what might have been a Pakistani accent, in response to some question of Kazuko Koike's. "That's just more or less black magic, you see." She put her hand on his shoulder and turned him right round—as if, like the gilded temple, he were mounted on a turntable —and enthusiastically pointed out to Miyake the particular way the man's robe was pleated behind. The fat priest and the thin came back, this time in pointed red hats, to close the dollhouse doors.

"Grand-u Smash-e! Grand-u Smash-e!" From the far side of the net, the tennis pro kept up a cannon fire of balls. A man a few steps ahead of me, dressed in a sweatshirt reading "Barbecue Club," swung his racquet determinedly, then wheeled off at a rapid trot to take his place at the back of the line of tennis students, for another round. Beyond the green mesh walls of the rooftop courts, Tokyo's dense and dun-colored outer boroughs stretched to the horizon, shimmering like a Sahara in the Sunday-morning sunshine. I stepped forward in my turn, dressed in an unmarked tracksuit borrowed from Jon Weiser, and made my swing, then circled off to line up again behind "Hello Sport," "Snoopy," "Woodstock," "Amusement Park," "Fisherman's Wharf," "Gut Is Heart of Racket," "Creativity," and "Emerson Football," who sprang, swung, wheeled, and trotted in conformity with the instructor's choreography. My itinerary had definitely speeded up.

"Japanese girls are small, with large faces and short legs," I had been told by a forceful young woman who had invited me along to share her lesson. She was a designer with a mass-market apparel company. "Issey and Yohji are for tall girls," she had said emphatically as she drove us across town to the courts. "Comme des Garçons is better for Japanese girls." She had rattled off the categories of the domestic fashion industry as she shifted gears: "European casual," "American casual," "career fashion," and the important class of "neutral fashion." (All these headings were in English.) The last kind, she had said, involved "adapting" Western designers "such as Perry Ellis," and thereby reaching the widest possible market. As we stood waiting for a traffic light to change, above us had loomed a billboard with a pert Japanese girl on the point of taking a large, roguish bite out of an Arby's roast-beef sandwich. (Changes in the Japanese diet have meant that many young women have longer and straighter legs than their mothers.) On the bus that waited alongside us I had noticed an English-language slogan that was part of another of the current saturation-advertising campaigns: "Be Sexy in Life!" A second bus, passing us with a roar and belch of fumes from the opposite direction, had carried the poster with the "HEALTHY" blonde holding up her silvery weight.

MORE than fifty percent of the population of Japan is under thirty. Most of the teen-age segment of that fifty percent seemed to be in Harajuku Park, dressed like the Fonz and his girl, and dancing some version of the Twist. As far as the eye could see, the broad paths were a squirming mass of thousands of figures dancing in sacred rings around huge cassette recorders and convocations of shopping bags. Youths in black leather motorcycle jackets—identical, save that some had "Tokyo Rockabilly Club" in a half-circle of white letters on the back—greeted arriving acquaintances with the flat-palm, "Yo, brother!" hand slap of Harlem, then resumed their dancing, with endlessly swivelling shoulders, knees, and feet. They smoked cigarettes in acutely stylized ways. Someone was always lifting an arm and crooking an elbow to pat or comb the side of a haircut, which was often topped with a spikily towering, electrified-looking Mohawk crest. One stupendously crested youth paused with his comb at the ready, absorbed by his own sharp-edged shadow unrolling on the path in a long, afternoon diagonal from out of his winklepicker shoes. An American man dressed, like the youths, in a black leather jacket, and with his hair in what looked by contrast like a very modest version of the greased-back Tony Curtis style, had edged himself into the fringe of the gyrating crowd. He was James Spina, the art director of *Women's Wear Daily;* in another context (as when I had seen him a few mornings earlier crossing the Okura's restaurant at the side of John Fairchild), he would have looked young and hip. As he detached himself from the crowd in the park and walked back to where Issey Miyake stood watching with Hebe Dorsey, the fashion editor of the *International Herald Tribune,* Spina appeared to have suffered a Dorian Gray–like shift into heavyset middle age. "That guy asked if I was a Hell's Angel," he said, shaking his head. "And he asked if I knew Queens. I gave him my Harley-Davidson badge. He seemed real pleased." He looked dazed at seeing so many versions of himself, so much his junior, and Japanese. "I've always dressed like this, as long as I can remember," he said, reaching inside his jacket and pulling out a cigarette.

There were armies of teen-age girls as well—sitting in tender and respectful circles around the dancing youths or dancing in sweet, stiff little lines of their own. Thousands and thousands of neon-colored chiffon-scarf bows puffed up and down on thousands of ponytails, and petticoated satin circle skirts swayed as their owners stepped, clapped, and hand-jived in close unison, lifting up and putting down dainty feet in lace-trimmed bobby socks and saddle shoes.

Hebe Dorsey gave a hitch to the neckline of her red cashmere poncho, with a sound of jangling from her many gold bracelets. "They are so amusing," she said.

Miyake had offered to take the Western visitors to this regular Sunday scene by car, and he was seeing it for the first time. He now stood by himself some way off, looking thoughtfully at the crowd, his elegant battle jacket slung over one shoulder. "Japanese people like very much to wear uniforms," he had said to me a few days earlier. "But when I began to work I wanted to show people how it is great to be free. I want to unwind the threads that bind them. If I feel myself the object of a cult, I skip away."

The boldest of a little group of teen-age girls wearing pedal pushers and white satin baseball jackets with the pink legend "White Fairies" greeted Miyake, after whisperings and gigglings. "Ah! Issey-san," she said.

We got into the car, and Hebe Dorsey began describing in detail the ball gown she had commissioned for the "Belle Epoque" gala in New York and talking about the Comtesse de Greffulhe and Liane de Pougy.

A line of Mohawk crests passed by on the sidewalk outside the car window, then a file of Cub Scouts, tripping along in bright-colored uniforms.

"I was so excited when I came here last year," Hebe Dorsey said.

On the way back to the hotel, we stopped at the Axis Building, where exquisitely tender modernity held sway. Even a store with bicycle wheels and motorcycle parts was arranged like a jewelry gallery in SoHo. In a tiny shop whose stock was a handful of pieces of modern furniture, a large red lacquer bowl rested on a low black table. "Ah, this bowl is beautiful," Miyake said, coming to life for the first time that afternoon.

From the folds of her red poncho Hebe Dorsey produced a small black camera.

In the bowl there rested a single shining chestnut and two whiskery ears of barley. Miyake took a step back, his head on one side. He removed the chestnut, looked at the bowl; put the chestnut back, looked at the bowl again.

"If only I could lug it," Hebe Dorsey said.

. . .

MANY members of the group who sat that evening at an L-shaped table in front of a spray of blossoms and a coromandel screen in the restaurant called Daini's Table were able to join, in one language or another, in comparisons of its Chinese nouvelle cuisine with that of the Mr. Chow in New York and with that of the original Mr. Chow, in London, too. Sonia Rykiel, who had arrived in a striking barrel-shaped coat of black marabou, like a funereal Big Bird suit, sat flanked by Issey Miyake and Kei Mori, Mme. Mori's younger son. Kei Mori runs his own fashion business, Studio V; he is a dapperly dressed man of such small stature that even his mother had commented on it (with affection), at our lunch. Ettore Sottsass, apparently recovered from his jet lag, and wearing a highly colored Russian Constructivist–style Memphis necktie, sat opposite. *"J'a-dore la publicité!"* he said, in Italian-accented French. He was to be photographed for a Seibu advertising-poster campaign, framed by a doorway he had designed specially. "That's why I'm so happy in Japan, always. The Japanese have no complexes about advertising, publicity—all that."

I said that there seemed something particularly compelling about the world of the Japanese advertisement.

He gave a jovial shrug. "Everything is relative," he said. "If you played Fellini in New Guinea, it might look perfectly natural."

Down the table, I could hear Selma Weiser complaining to Daini, a suave young man in a boldly striped Savile Row suit, who was of the party, about the impenetrable street addresses of Tokyo. "Little maps! 'Second pine tree from the corner, turn left'! I don't think people in this town want other people to find them."

Sonia Rykiel and Issey Miyake were talking about being recognized on the street. "I'm a redhead, so people have turned to stare at me my whole life," Sonia Rykiel said.

Little delicacy followed little delicacy; little dish, little dish. Litchi nuts appeared. Sonia Rykiel was rubbing her collarbone and talking about the new Japanese fashions. "But these clothes don't touch the body," she said. "They float around it. I think these designers are afraid of the body."

Ettore Sottsass saw what she meant. "The way their shoe barely touches the foot," he said, using his hands to illustrate a single toe thong, a sole tenuously attached.

Some people were rising to leave.

Sonia Rykiel threw her arms round Miyake and reminded him of a weekend they had spent as fellow house guests on the Île de Ré, in France.

"It was *wonderful,*" he said.

Makiko Minagawa, in an indigo-and-white cotton kimono, sat a few seats off, smiling to herself. Jon Weiser was standing behind his sister's chair, massaging her shoulders. Miyake sat in front of lacquered golden cranes on a black screen. His hands were circling, his eyes were sparkling. "Tokyo and New York are very close together at the moment, I feel," he said.

JAMES Spina, generally known as Jimmy, rose from where he had been watching the time-around-the-world map and walked with me to the stationery store. "I love hotel lobbies," he said. "But when I stayed at the Ritz to cover the shows in Paris the concierge made me use the Rue Cambon entrance if I was going to dress in my way." He walked along with his hands plunged in the two vertical pockets of his motorcycle jacket. From the billboards and walls of stores on the Ginza, house-high photographs of "real people," models, and "personalities," both Oriental and Occidental, stared down at us or laughed their heads off over some gargantuan private joke. "I had to buy a tux specially for this trip," he said. "I only ever had one good suit. It's blue, with that great loose-fitting look. I've had it for seventeen years, and it was my father's when he got out of the Army. But he hardly ever wore it, because he grew a potbelly right away. My dad's a carpenter. Worked all his life in Long Island City. Near where my friend Tina Weymouth has a loft. You know Tina? The Talking Heads?" We stopped for a cup of coffee. The menu was densely laminated, with Technicolor photographs of ice-cream sundaes. "I always like when you can order by pointing at photographs," Jimmy Spina said. He reached inside the front of his jacket for a cigarette. He had gone to high school in Queens, had a good Catholic upbringing, had even been an altar boy—the whole bit. Mr. Fairchild had had to go back to New York; often personally wrote the gossip in *Women's Wear* signed "Louise J. Esterhazy"; was a genius; had advised Spina to bring along his penny loafers, because they were easily slipped on and off at the entrance to tatami-matted rooms.

"SEXY!" Issey Miyake said. "Always they ask me, 'What is "sexy"?' " The young woman reporter from *Asahi*'s magazine *Footwork,* who had earlier posed that question to Sonia Rykiel, Norma Kamali, Valentino, Kansai, and Mme. Mori, had just left the Miyake Design Studio. Miyake was still sitting behind his big, modern, blond-wood desk, which was bare except for an Olivetti agenda, a coffee-table book about Canada, and a cup of green tea. He made a rueful face, stretching out his hands. "I think Japanese people still find it hard to talk about these things," he said, sighing. Behind him on the white wall, a light-and-shade texture made by horizontal wood strips like music staffs set off his black shirt—a special Miyake collarless style, comfortably unbuttoned. "I say to her that it should not be a question—that only adult people, with their personality, can understand the word. She asks me, 'Is sexy the same as "healthy"?'

I say, 'Beautiful teeth, hair, eyes—that *helps.*' But I say to her, 'How can you express beauty in words? It is for that I am working. You can express "healthy" easily, but not beauty.'" His head turned in profile, in front of two copies of the Trisha Brown upraised-arm photograph pinned on a bulletin board next to the strips of wood. He stretched out his own arm, unconsciously echoing the dancer's pose. Sunshine streamed into the room, passing through the winged white petals of a moth-orchid and spilling in ribbons on the straw rug. "I say to her, "Sometimes the sky is very sexy. And flowers. And water. Or even a large crowd.'" He furrowed his brow, looked upward, then down. "Like this, I try to explain to her a little bit. I think she understands." Behind him, too, were the turtle and the snake and a photograph of what looked from where I sat like female mud-wrestlers.

"SHE is so pleased you asked about the holes," said Stella Ishii, who was serving as interpreter for Rei Kawakubo, of Comme des Garçons. "Through you, we are able to explain this to your readers. And when Bernadine Morris, of *The New York Times,* was here, earlier, we were very happy that she asked about the makeup for our show in Paris. Many people misunderstood, said the models looked somehow—well, *bruised,* or *battered.*" Stella Ishii was a young woman with wire-rimmed glasses and with long hair in a severe-looking bun at the nape. She was dressed all in black, and looked more like the designer's disciple than her business manager, which was what she was. We were sitting in a windowless room with gray-painted concrete walls and floor, bare except for two large black leather sofas, a huge, square, black leather club chair, and a photographer's lamp that looked as though it would have sufficient wattage for a night ballgame if it were to be illuminated. Rei Kawakubo sat facing me, seated in the black leather chair as on a throne. She was a small, slight woman dressed in a black tunic-style dress over long underwear–style black pants. She wore her dark hair in a short pageboy bob with thick, full bangs overhanging a face devoid of makeup. (This abstention from cosmetics had seemed striking enough to both Miss Suita and Miss Minagawa for each of them to tell me of it when the designer's name came up.) Rei Kawakubo watched my face as I asked my questions and as Miss Ishii translated them into Japanese, at what seemed like four times their length. Rei Kawakubo sat very upright, her small, black-shod feet placed neatly side by side and flat on the floor. Her forearms rested squarely along the wide leather arms of her chair. When she had understood a question and was ready to give her answer, or when she wished to signify its completion, her hands lifted fractionally and her eyelids, under the black bangs, dropped shut and then opened again. Sometimes, as she began a sentence her head tilted to one side and she made tremulous humming sounds. There was a half-open door behind her right shoulder, with a source of light somewhere. Huge, distorted shadow people passed across this rectangle in silence from time to time.

I asked Rei Kawakubo why she used so much black and gray.

Miss Ishii interpreted.

Rei Kawakubo hummed, uttered, fell silent again. The eyelids went up and down, the little, pale hands lifted and settled again.

"She sees enough colors in life," Miss Ishii said.


THE taxicab moved up from the head of the curbside stand. Its door popped open. The commissionaire of the Okura ushered me into the cab. "Hanae Mori Building?" he said, with a grin, as he shut the door.


"JAPAN doesn't have any competition in fashion at the moment—it's doing something so different, the way it did with hi-fi. This is fashion thoroughly informed by traditional aesthetics: *aji,* which might involve fabrics where the incongruity speaks of the congruity of the whole; the idea of sleeves filled with nothing; the idea of colored space, as in Edo Kabuki." Donald Richie, an American who has lived for many years in Tokyo and is a scholarly expert on such subjects as Noh, Zen, and Japanese cinema, was sitting in one of the Breuer chairs in the street-level coffee shop of the Hanae Mori Building. Across the aisle was a boutique where "H.M."– initialled silk neckties and pastel umbrellas lay arranged in quintessentially Japanese displays from the hand of Robert Currie. Richie had close-cropped graying hair and a refreshingly unfashionable jacket of olive-drab corduroy. In rare pauses in his talk, he leaned back with folded arms and bounced gently on his chair or refilled his cigarette holder, sticking it back between his teeth at the angle customarily called "rakish." "So much of our fashion in the West has to do with Warhol attitudes by now," he said. "With subtle putting down of things. But Japan is a country where you can't, in our sense, 'read' anything."

I had come to our meeting primed to ask Richie about his "appearance and reality" theory.

"Appearance *is* the reality here," he said now, before I had had a chance to prompt him. "The ostensible is the real. There is no single word for 'hypocritical' in the Japanese language. No single word for 'ironic,' either. There's plenty of humor here but no real wit. And no cynicism. This is a very pragmatic country. What works is good; what doesn't work is bad. And, no matter how hard you look, the mask *is* the face. There is no notion of 'the real me,' a being somehow separate from the person. People here are what you can see, constructed from the outside. In spite of what they say, there's no real religion except the religion of being Japanese. The pattern for success is to go abroad, achieve some recognition, and come back straight away. Two years is good, five years not so good. If you stay too long, it's considered a bad thing. You lose your Japaneseness. You've left the tribe."

I said to him, as I had tried to say to Ettore Sottsass, that the dimensions of image, celebrity, and advertising—of Seibu's Woody Allen and of "East Meets West"—seemed particularly haunting.

Richie nodded vigorously. "The Japanese take what is well known and emblematic in the West and *own* it," he said. "And it's not a question of their being 'plastic' people, because everything here is 'plastic.' Of course, it is we who are living a falsehood in the West, with our absurd idea of 'the real me,' with our 'strong beliefs.' Oh, no! Plato and Saint Paul really led us astray! And the Renaissance, of course. *Everything* here is presentational."

The glass doors of the Hanae Mori Building swung open, and Sonia Rykiel came sweeping in, wearing a long black cape. A worried-looking, very correctly dressed Japanese man followed, carrying the designer's capacious holdall. After him came Nathalie Rykiel, in her Japanese-peasant costume. As they headed for the escalator at our elbow, I greeted Sonia Rykiel and introduced Richie. She perched on an empty chair at our table while her group sailed upward to The Space without her. "We have been talking about the new Japanese style," I said. She continued some of the thoughts she had shared with Sottsass at Daini's, and said that because of having been bound in kimonos, and so on, the Japanese were afraid to show the body. "They are making these clothes for foreign women," she said.

Donald Richie had been watching her fixedly and in silence. His expression combined that of a man trying hard to follow sentences in French with that of a man who might just possibly have been the sole inventor and guardian of the English word "ironic." He leaned forward with a sudden movement, snatching his cigarette holder out from between his teeth. "What amazing hair!" he said to Sonia Rykiel. "Do you dye it?"

"Of course, the guiding passion—the hedonistic, decadent demand

—in the West is for constant novelty," he went on smoothly after Mme. Rykiel had gathered her cape about her and soared off up the escalator. "It's a form of bankruptcy. The Zen boom—boomlet, shall we say—to which I have contributed my modest share by writing my books is a sign of this bankruptcy. So is the idea of the new celibacy. Instead of going to bed with each other, people have to go back to holding hands, because that's the only thing that's sexy now. And the taste for this sort of fashion is another sign of bankruptcy. If society is a big lobster ambling slowly along on the bottom of the ocean, fashion is the antennae sticking out in front." He squinted waggishly out through the smoke that rose from his cigarette, and waved his two forefingers from side to side, like feelers.

NORMA Kamali is the first fashion designer of recent times to have achieved an international reputation without giving a single fashion show. The presentation in The Space at the Hanae Mori Building was to be her first. I squeezed past the knees of Sonia Rykiel to reach a seat left in the front row of the bleachers.

"Mr. Richie has been telling me about Japan," I said.

"I hope he wasn't telling you all wrong," Sonia Rykiel said.

I sat between Jimmy Spina and Kei Mori. We were a bright-colored, spaghetti-spined line compared with the rest of the audience—predominantly gray-suited men, once more, with their hands resting on their knees. Down the line, Norma Kamali's foot in its high-heeled boot was swaying next to Kansai's combat boot in time to the opening music. The video image of Norma Kamali blossomed once again all over The Space. "Spare me," the real Norma Kamali said, with a groan. Bright nineteen-fifties circle skirts came out with off-the-shoulder tops. Music was peppy nineteen-fifties style, its lyrics filled with double-entendres. Jimmy Spina's eyes shone; once or twice, he let rip with a whistle. A blond girl with fluffy tendrils of hair pretended to tumble over backward in a red prom dress, disappearing in a froth of white net Harajuku petticoats. Thin young women and slender young men in dramatically revealing bathing suits or leotards pretended to lift weights or swim. People crawled across the floor. The scantily clad men converged on a solitary scantily clad woman. "In New York City and in Detroit, too," bopped the song. Jimmy Spina was holding on to the two ends of his red muffler and bouncing his fists up and down on his black leather chest in time to the music. Kamali denims had a *West Side Story* theme. "When you're a Jet, you're a Jet . . ." ran the soundtrack. "When you're a Jet you're a Jet all the way, from your first cigarette . . ." Jimmy Spina knew all the words by heart, sang along, looking quite transported. Then (after the denim-clad group had pretended to shoot someone to death) the little black toddler was onstage again, with her tweaks of hair and dungarees, jumping up and down and dispensing loose-wristed waves with her dimpled hand. And the red balloons were out again, in force; and a pregnant woman was walking on (to lend a real touch); and the handsome young men were pretending to be family men, with children in their bodybuilders' arms; and American flags were waving to and fro; and "The Battle Hymn of the Republic" was ringing out; and Norma Kamali's face was back on all the screens again; and the gray-suited men were sitting with fists on knees, watching.

ONE of the black models, looking ten feet tall, walked between the tables of the coffee shop and out of the door in her street clothes, with some calla lilies on the crook of her arm. Issey Miyake waved wanly at Makiko Minagawa as he hurried limpingly away from the Kamali show. "He is a little tired right now, a little agitated," Makiko Minagawa said, following him with her eyes. "He must look after so many foreign women."

It had started to rain. The restaurant that Makiko Minagawa and I went to was unpretentious, as cozy as the inside of an overcoat pocket. "I think Norma Kamali's clothes are good if you have beautiful Western body," Makiko Minagawa said. "Japanese body not beautiful."

Soup arrived to terminate the meal. Why was my soup dark while hers was pale?

Makiko Minagawa nodded in the direction of the proprietor, a hefty woman dressed in the style favored by Nathalie Rykiel, and standing with arms akimbo behind the counter looking down at me with amusement. "She say foreign people like to eat mushrooms."

As I lay sleepless beside the active blue digits (for my jet lag had reawakened and was all set to come along when I left Japan), I thought about Norma Kamali and her show. I remembered an afternoon spent with Norma Kamali and some other people. Was it five years ago, or six, or seven? The man whose apartment we were in had one of those Mylar racing-driver jackets; he wouldn't have been caught dead in it any later. Mick and Bianca Jagger must still have been married to each other, too, because their personalities were discussed at length. Our host had a parrot in a cage by the window, squawking and spitting husks of seeds into Norma Kamali's hair. He had a bathroom with quadraphonic-sound speakers in it for his Gregorian chants, and some far stranger things than that in it as well. He played us a tape of himself being analyzed by a psychic who lived in Brooklyn. There was a coil of incense on the window-sill. It gave off tiny puffs of smoke like smoke signals. The sky was unbelievably blue; then it turned that amazing turquoise green. There was the Empire State Building. People looked up at it from time to time as they lay with their elbows on cushions, talking about acupuncture and past lives, and drinking Lapsang souchong. One man there was sitting on a little upholstered bench. He was quite obsessed by Versailles. "Imagine the early-morning mist. The *bassins,*" he said. He went on and on about the King. "He was perfect," he said. "The only mistake he made in his whole life was when some courtier he had banished came back and danced the dance that had been in fashion when he went away. The King laughed. But that was the only mistake he ever made in his entire *life.*"

I got out of bed. The sky was charcoal gray, with teeming rain. A ferocious wind was blowing. The Rising Sun atop the Nippon Mining Company was soaking wet and stiff, like a flag made of metal. The parking lot under my window filled up like a lake: a lost undersea civilization to which boxlike white lines and arrows provided no-longer-meaningful clues. Bright-gold leaves spun wildly over gray-black waters that began to form themselves into waves. Water gushed from the Okura's gutters, rocketing and crashing down into the parking-lot lake, where now a solitary unmarked truck came forging along like a tugboat, with arcs of water splashing out at fender height. A man in streaming black oilskins lifted the back tarpaulin and unloaded dozens and dozens of large green wreaths.

# THE LIGHT
# IN THE EYE

THE honeybee buzzed and plunged into a foxglove bell. The London *Times* slipped off my knee and rustled onto the lawn. I was in England during that strangest of English summers—1981. For weeks, the nation's television screens had been as gay as computer games, with petrol bombs and policemen's helmets flying about in riot-torn inner-city nights. Next, everyone was out in Hyde Park for Handel and fireworks, and (lo!) the Royal Wedding of Charles and Di came on the television screens at last. I had been reading about the British photographer Norman Parkinson as I sat dozing in my garden chair. He was to have a big show—fifty years' worth of his fashion photographs and his portraits of personages lovely, famous, rich, or royal—at the National Portrait Gallery, in London. Alongside photographs by Parkinson (women golfing at Le Touquet in 1939; Montgomery Clift scratching his eyebrow in New York in 1952), the newspaper reproduced a photograph *of* Parkinson. He was manifestly a personage in his own right, seen striding through tropic greenery wearing a sort of Byronic cricketing outfit, a big snow-white last-days-of-Empire mustache, and what looked like a Victorian smoking cap. I was to learn that Parkinson was sixty-eight years old and six feet, five inches tall, that he had been christened Ronald William Parkinson Smith, and that many people called him Parks. When he was not busy photographing lovely, famous, rich, or royal people all over the world, these days, he was running a pig farm and sausage-making factory, producing "Porkinson's Bangers," on the Caribbean Island of Tobago, where he had made his home for the past twenty years. He was rather fed up with photographing fashion models by now, he told his interviewer from the *Times.* The new

Princess of Wales was still away on her honeymoon, on the royal yacht, but Parkinson said he would like to photograph her really soon, before she lost her lovely bloom.


"I'M A bit of an expert on bloom, as a matter of fact," Parkinson said, lifting the big, starched napkin to give each end of his mustache a raffish wipe.

Over a year had passed, and he and I were lunching in a restaurant, one winter day, in New York. ("Shall we be really silly and go to Le Cirque?" he had said. "If they let me sit where I usually sit, it's a great place for *staring*.") He settled knife and fork on his empty plate and leaned back on the banquette with an air of satisfaction. Without the smoking cap, his head proved large, well shaped, and—save for a narrow tonsure ring of hair as snowy as the mustache—completely bald. He was dressed in a young-Chatterton linen shirt (the maître d' had waved aside with a pained expression Mr. Parkinson's question whether he might, like other men patrons, be called upon to wear a tie) and a linen suit with broad brown and olive stripes which was either inordinately ugly or spectacularly full of style.

"Bloom," he said, exhaling the word like smoke from a fine cigar. "Ah, *yes*. Hangs about a face before it's been exposed. Occasionally, you find people who still have bloom at forty or fifty, you know. What do you think of this Chablis?" He made a swirling motion with a chain-braceleted wrist. The wine mounted the inside of the glass in a sheet of gold, fell undulating back.

At tables all around ours, faces kept swivelling to the door at the sound of new arrivals, then huddling close together again, confidential in the petal light from hothouse flowers. Women's hands, heavy with diamonds, stirred coffee in tiny cups or alighted playfully on a neighboring sleeve. Young men's hands, with costly cufflinks and the slimmest of watches, waved languorously at wine buckets and waiters.

"What were those little eggs, Romeo?" Parkinson said, looking up as a hand came reaching out to take his plate. "Plover? Quail?" He had just come back from the White House and a sitting with Mrs. Ronald Reagan. "I've been looking at the transparencies, and it seems I've made her look like a girl of twenty-one," he said, with a grin. "Except for the hands, of course. Always give the game away, the hands." Security had been tight. "Specially trained dogs, sniffin' at one. Remarkable, really." Playfully, he tossed an imaginary rubber ball in the air ("That's how the trainers set them off") and did a perfect imitation of a dog ("A young bitch was assigned to me; I was lucky") snuffling with eager nostrils after potentially explosive clues.

As an apprentice in London at the start of the nineteen-thirties, Parkinson learned all about producing portraits of debutantes who came along to the studio of Speaight & Son wearing long white gowns, long white gloves, and white feather head-pinnings (as their mothers and grandmothers had before them) after curtsying as they were presented to the King and Queen. "Speaight was a court photographer, not a society photographer," Parkinson said, once he had discussed and then ordered Le Cirque's crème brûlée. "There was a cunning difference. 'Society' was about as nasty a word as 'fashion' in those days." Then he had set up on his own in Dover Street, producing portraits and fashion shots, working for magazines such as *The Bystander,* and covering Noël Coward's garden party and Edward VIII's famous tour of Depression-bound Wales.

Sometimes, with Norman Parkinson, there is the impression of a self-protective click, a puff of photographer's smoke that lets him skip out of reach behind a jovial double. "I was a photographer and a farmer," he said from behind his double when I asked about the Second World War. "Most of the officers of the brigade I would have joined were killed at Dunkirk, so perhaps it was just as well." That he was a conscientious objector is one of several speculations, most of them well-meaning, that acquaintances hold about him. ("It may sound a silly thing to say," Parkinson says, "but I don't think I have many enemies.")

Along with the war came Condé Nast. Parkinson's passionate relationship with British *Vogue* lasted for over thirty years, until it was shaken by a bitter dispute with Condé Nast over copyrights. ("A photographer without a magazine behind him is like a farmer without fields," he says.) In the late forties, Parkinson also began selling work to American *Vogue;* for a decade, he spent part of each year in the United States. "What was it carved on the wall at the old Idlewild?" he said.

" 'Bring me your tired, your starvin' poor . . .' " Parkinson was dangling his silvery teaspoon perpendicular, its tip teasing the fragile crust of his crème brûlée. It was hard to imagine him as any kind of huddled mass. "I was the tiniest bit huddled in those days, actually," he said, allowing his spoon to plunge into the cream.

HUDDLED or not, in the times when Parkinson was at home in the rationed Britain of the late forties and early fifties he produced what purists regard as the finest work of his career. Like the Princess of Wales, Parkinson's photographs had their big moment of bloom. (By the spring of 1983, Parkinson was telling the magazine *People* that although Her Royal Highness had had a tremendous share of that commodity she seemed to have lost it singularly fast.) When his work was assembled and sorted for the first time, for the National Portrait Gallery show (all his prewar negatives had been lost in the blitz; some later prints lay forgotten in Twickenham, where Parkinson has kept a London pied-à-terre), it was the forties and fifties photographs that seemed fresh and clear—windows open on an England vanished, shimmering, and non-Americanized. Here was London as an exclusive, insiders' city, unfolding itself after the years of war. Squares, churches, railings, self-confident, dandified men in bowlers, and fragile, feminine women in New Look skirts stood out as if new-minted against a radiant, misty air. Parkinson's countryside bloomed, too. Here were pony carts and picnic hampers, stiles and sensible shoes, gaitered yokels and shove-ha'penny boards in old pub parlors, branch-line stations and steam trains, and hedgerows overflowing with meadowsweet. At the heart of it all, as like as not, there was a beautiful little face with a look that seemed to hover perpetually between sadness and fun: the face of Wenda Rogerson, who was then Parkinson's favorite model, and who has been his wife for the past forty-odd years.

"I'VE been mad for King Ludwig of Bavaria ever since Blunt's book came out," Parkinson said, referring to Wilfrid Blunt's *The Dream King*. Parkinson was in New York often in the winter and early spring of 1983. On one of his meteorlike passages through town, he had invited me to his hotel room, high up above Central Park, on a day when the light was like a gray eiderdown puffed out with impending snow. His aluminum camera cases stood ready, softly gleaming, by the door. He was wearing a flowing white shirt, girdled at hip level with gold-metal X shapes; a necklace with little figures of naked women; and trousers that looked, on his heronlike legs, like terrycloth long johns. He was showing me some transparencies—not of Nancy Reagan, to be sure (for he would shield an unretouched first lady as diplomatically as a queen), but of Mrs. Gordon Getty. She was a redhead. Festooned in a series of magnificent gowns and jewels, and cornered in the baroque exuberance of the Mad Monarch's castles at Linderhof and Herrenchiemsee, she looked distinctly highstrung.

"April *Town & Country*," Parkinson murmured, screwing a magnifying viewer to his eye and quizzing his efforts with some satisfaction. As he sat by the window with the smudgy snow-light on his brow, he looked like an Englishman in an eighteenth-century painting. In the real world down below, tiny figures in bright tracksuits ran round and round the bare gray park, looping under leafless trees. With thumb and forefinger Parkinson held out a transparency. I took it from him and held it between my eyes and the light. Mrs. Getty was standing there inside the little white frame wearing wild-looking hair and flinging out an arm toward a cockle-shell boat that floated in an artificial grotto.

"Ludwig loved swans, as you know," Parkinson said, handing me a second slide. There was a painted swan, and a stuffed one, and Mrs. Getty dressed something like a swan as well.

"And peacocks." In another photograph, Mrs. Getty looked something like a peacock.

There followed an extravaganza of frescoes, cherubs, mirrors, flickering candles, rococo gilding, yet another make-believe bird. Mrs. Getty was seated at an ornate instrument, a mating of a piano and a harmonium —it looked a little like a wedding cake—and pretending, with a look of wary ecstasy, to rest her head on its keys. "My most Wagnerian," Parkinson said. "See what I mean about this being a good moment for a return to *style*?"

PARKINSON planned to be in New York again in April, to mount an exhibition of his work at Sotheby's; celebrate his seventieth birthday; and launch the book *Fifty Years of Style and Fashion,* a selection of his photographs with an autobiographical text. His schedule, habitually frantic, became even more so as the triple event approached. "Threescore years and ten, and one has so *much* still to do," he said around this time. "You have to get the whip out when you're into the last furlong." He flew from New York to London, commissioned by *The Tatler* to photograph Koo Stark, a young woman whose relationship with Prince Andrew, the Queen's second son, had fuelled the Fleet Street gossip machines for some time, not least because her brief career as an actress had included a role in distinctly dubious taste. ("The Earl of Pembroke and a fellow called Chalky White put her in a little film," Parkinson told me before he left for London. "A sort of fantasy, you might say. Then the media dubbed her a porno star. Not enough breast to fill a thimble; no real beauty; but a sweet girl, very bright.") He flew back to New York and photographed some models. ("Who would have thought, after fifty years of snappin', that the ultimate accolade would be not to do the Royals but to do a catalogue for Bloomingdale's?" he once said.) He flew home to the Caribbean to attend carnival in Trinidad, as usual. "I got suitably pixillated," he said when he came back to New York again. "I like to shed my skin of privacy at least once a year." He flew off to London once more, to photograph what he called "some minor Royals."

"I find I get tired more easily in London," Parkinson says. In New York, his energy always seems boundless. "People are so full of envy there—they're always *fencing* with one, like in *The Three Musketeers.* In America, they *like* success, they embrace it."

He flew back to New York and accepted the *Times Magazine*'s commission to photograph a number of men designers, including Calvin Klein. He photographed some women, among them Mrs. Harry Helmsley, wife of the real-estate owner, posing in gorgeous gowns behind the scenes at the hotels she runs and pretending to be a queen. ("Women always get into the spirit of a sitting so much better than men," he said. "They say, 'Would you like me to try another dress, Mr. Parkinson, or different jewels?'") He hired a public-relations expert to help promote his book —"to play John the Baptist for two or three months," he said—and then ran a good P.R. campaign for himself, of the kind that doesn't seem to try. He lunched at Le Cirque again, and talked a lot more about bloom. He folded his long legs into the limousine used by *Town & Country* and raced here and there around New York. Murray Cohen was generally the driver on these trips. "I love fashion," Mr. Cohen said to me once. "Used to be in the cloak-and-suit trade myself. I don't always understand the way the guy dresses, if you get what I'm saying. But that Mr. Parkinson, he's a real gentleman."

PARKINSON'S bald pate was like a calendar, announcing how long he had been gone from his home—a house that (if he does say so himself) is one of the most beautiful houses in the Caribbean, and from whose bedroom window (on a clear day) he can see Venezuela. After time spent in Tobago, his head was a polished chestnut brown; after time spent in London or New York, its color faded, and freckles stood out on it like speckles on the belly of a trout. By mid-April, and the gala dinner for the exhibition of his work at Sotheby's, the pate was at its palest as he stood in the receiving line and inclined it toward arriving guests. Each invitation card bore a copy of Parkinson's most famous portrait of recent years—the triple study of the Queen, the Queen Mother, and Princess Margaret, who had all got into the spirit by agreeing to dress up in blue satin capes and match exactly, as though they were the Supremes. The portentous glamour of "Royal Blue Trinity," with its suggestion of a Royal Command, was a nice Parkinsonian touch; it was actually *Town & Country* that was picking up the evening's tab. In the receiving line, Parkinson, in black velvet coat, striped trousers, and wing collar, was quasi-paternal in his greeting to Jerry Hall, the Texas fashion model, in her black velvet dress; quasi-paternal, too, with Koo Stark, the very bright girl, in her black lace. He was courtly and gentle with middle-aged society women and hail-fellow hearty with a covey of Peers of the Realm who had just arrived in town from London (except for His Grace the Duke of Marlborough, who was suntanned from a stay in Palm Beach) to publicize "Britain Salutes New York," the British Arts Festival. Having upstaged the next evening's official festival opening with his more glittering event, Parkinson, in the days to come, would remain relatively aloof from that group promotion of British culture. After all, hadn't he imported his individual Englishness (highly wrought, and somewhat under aspic, like the late David Niven's) successfully enough for years?

Norman Parkinson hates, above all, to be bored. Hand after hand came out to shake his hand. Ball gowns kept on emerging from limousines and floating toward him up the stairs. Wenda Parkinson, whose face still wears its look of mingled sadness and fun, stood beside her husband in the line. He greeted another arriving stranger and waved in Wenda Parkinson's direction. "I don't believe you've met my mistress," he said to the stranger, and the stranger looked surprised.

"Parkinson won't let me have a face-lift," Wenda Parkinson says from time to time. Many of the arriving faces were as taut as masks. These were faces that had been made into photographs very often in the past; some of them were in Parkinson's prints, hanging on the walls. These were faces that would without exception be photographed again before the night was out, for each male escort would receive a loaded Polaroid camera as a favor, between the first course and the entrée. These were faces that seemed two-dimensional, like photographs, now, as they circled the rooms diplomatically exchanging mutual visibilities.

"You look gorgeous, as always," said one, with a little stiff bow.

"Doesn't Betsy look divine tonight?" said the other, by way of a reply. Glances and astringent kisses buzzed about.

I walked around the rooms.

Item (hanging on the wall): Various portraits of Wenda Parkinson when young, including Wenda thumbnail-size in front of a great waterfall in Natal, in 1951.

Item (framed, on top of the grand piano, along with some candelabras): Princess Anne on a cantering horse.

Item (framed, on the wall nearby): Princess Anne with a diamond tiara on highly teased hair; a fluffy white fur wrap; and a face dramatically contoured by elaborate makeup.

Item (on the wall): A red-haired young woman followed by two Italian dwarfs in cap and bells.

Item (in person): Leona Helmsley in a dress with sleeves like Lurex water wings.

Item (on the wall): Leona Helmsley in pink organza.

Item (on the wall): Miss Piggy.

Item (on the wall): The Queen Mother photographed through rain-spotted glass and with shafts of light shooting out from her diamonds.

Item (on the wall): Elizabeth Taylor (ditto).

Item (on the wall): Mrs. Reagan, with young-looking hands.

Item (on the wall): The fashion model Carmen Dell'Orefice (known simply as Carmen) wearing a bikini and waist-length black hair on a beach in the Bahamas, in 1959.

Item (in person): Carmen with silver hair standing straight up from her narrow face in a Mme. de Pompadour–wig effect, and wearing a crinoline ringed with coq feathers. ("The dress is Michaele Vollbracht," I heard someone say. "Can you believe she's *fifty-two*?")

Item (on the wall, and on the cover of Parkinson's new book): Iman Haywood, the Somali model, and Jerry Hall, the Texas one, wearing dark fur hats and with their cheeks together.

Item (in person): Iman Haywood and Jerry Hall sitting at a table with Apollonia van Ravenstein, another model, and with Iman's husband, Spencer Haywood—a bearded, six-foot, nine-inch black man from Detroit, in transition between careers as a basketball star and as a business-man and occasional model.

Item (on the wall): Jerry Hall wearing extravagant jewels and em-bracing her boyfriend, Mick Jagger, both parties bare to the waist.

Item (on the wall): The Parkinsons' son, Simon, as an angelic five-year-old with pale-blond hair.

Item (in person): Simon Parkinson as a thirty-seven-year-old man, the owner of a restaurant in Port of Spain, Trinidad, and of a Polaroid camera, which he is busily directing at the gathering.

Item (on the wall): The newspaper gossip columnist Aileen Mehle (Suzy) wearing a kind of diamond swimming cap, scanty classical drap-eries, and a tremulous expression.

Item (in person): The television celebrity-interviewer Nikki Haskell, in a strapless gown, arranging people for interviews in front of their portraits in a beatifying blaze of camera lights.

Item (on the wall): Barbara Cartland, the romantic novelist, in full fig, together with her Pekinese.


"OH, I know what they always say about me," Parkinson told me once. " 'Why is that chap Parkinson always so *weak*?' But, really, what ever is the point of weaseling one's way into Mrs. Astor's and then making her look like a hobgoblin? When I look through the camera, I see an aura about people, a joy and a gaiety about it all. The camera can be the most deadly weapon since the assassin's bullet. Or it can be the lotion of the heart."

I asked how he felt about photographing people he didn't like.

"I don't believe I've ever had to do it," he said.

Now Parkinson was bounding with high-lifted knees across the dance floor at Sotheby's to take the microphone after dinner. He likes making speeches—"getting on his legs," as Anthony Trollope would have said.

"I'm a tear-jerked old man," he said. "I've never seen a snapper— and that's *all* I am, you know—given an occasion like tonight's." He made some remarks about success and failure, and told a story about a cockerel and some ducks on a farmyard pond. "I won't go on and on, like Dickie Attenborough at the Oscars," he said. "I'm not for peace! I'm for beauty!" The invited crowd in evening dress ("You dear, good, kind people in America," Parkinson had called them), seated round tables littered with Polaroid images of itself, lifted ring after ring of flushed, pale, or painted faces at these remarks and let out a roar.

"WITH Parkinson, there's none of that nonsense photographers cling to about the difference between their commercial and their artistic work," one observer said at the Sotheby's show. "It's *all* his 'real' work. That way, he never opens the door for anyone to judge him. There are probably as many different Parkinsons on these walls as there are magazines he has sold to. But then who's to say that everyone should be like Avedon and have everything you do look like an Avedon?" Lucrative careers doing what Parkinson calls "reaping the harvest of fashion" have led some photographers to look hard at uncommercial images of ugliness, age, and death as well. There are rumors that Parkinson has a private collection of photographs of freaks and physical deformities, but his public work has generally involved an unflinching gaze at generations of beauties or the patient wait for that flash of light on the tiara. (It is tempting, though, to see Parkinson's flattery—that of his recent portraits, especially—as a veiled contempt. It is as if he embraced his starry-eyed subjects and slowly hugged them to a high-camp, Technicolor death.) "Parkinson never looks back," people say. "He's always thinking about the next shot." He has seen wave after wave of youth and beauty. "I always think when models go to make a movie after six or seven years they've only got the fag end of their looks," he says. He was a star participant—along with David Bailey and Lord Snowdon, and other photographers far younger than he—in the booming visual birth of "Swinging London," in the late fifties and early sixties. For *Queen,* the liveliest of the period's glossy magazines, he photographed haute-couture fashions out of helicopters and in mountains and deserts far away. He took the portraits of the Rolling Stones as striplings and the Beatles with their bloom. In 1963, he left England and its tax system, thinking he would retire to Tobago and fish and swim. "But I wasn't as rich as I thought," he told me once, "and the first time a fashion editor sent a telegram saying 'Sending model with twenty bathing suits' I was off again, like a shot." (This most jet-setting of men has lived without a telephone at home for more than twenty years.)

"The age of real fashion, big fashion, died with Dior," he says. "These models now, they fly in and out; they get their two thousand dollars a day, then they give you the same photograph they gave the chap who did them yesterday. There's no such thing as real beauty anymore —just the face that takes the makeup best. All these hairdressers and makeup men, they're all still playing with dolls, really. I suppose *I'm* still playing with dolls, come to that. Even at my age, I find I'm still attracted to the models. It's like the mongoose and the snake, to get a shot. A rhythm springs up; it can go for an hour, an hour and a half. Then, suddenly, that girl will give you something—a little shrug, a look, something. You've got to take it then. If she gave it and you didn't take it, you'd lose her. I have a passion for the opposite sex. I like the way they look at themselves in shopwindows—all that. One knows the way their *muscles* work. I suppose you could say that's how I came to get involved, as I did, with breeding race horses."

·   ·   ·

PARKINSON'S book went bobbing along on its maiden voyage through New York, alongside the more stately progress of the "Britain Salutes New York" festival. He continued to publicize himself most affably. "They've given me a bell and a tricorne hat and a pair of rather down-at-heel shoes," he said, describing his efforts, "and I'm kept busy doing the old 'Oyez! Oyez!' " Bloomingdale's gave a little tea party in his honor in the sixth-floor restaurant decorated like a Pullman car. The British Consul, Carmen, Iman, and Apollonia van Ravenstein held teacups while Parkinson got on his legs to thank "dear Bloomers" and allude to Noël Coward and his talent to amuse. Afterward, the Parkinsons went down in the elevator with Terence Pepper, the curator of photographs at Britain's National Portrait Gallery, who had helped mount Parkinson's New York show at Sotheby's as well as the earlier, English one. The doors opened on the main floor next to some pompous-looking display cases crammed, in honor of the Anglophile moment, with an assortment of royal memorabilia. American citizens with shopping bags passed incuriously to and fro in front of black-bordered cards to "Admit Bearer to the Quadrangle" of Windsor Castle for the funerals of monarchs, or china struck to show support of Queen Caroline against the Prince Regent.

"Rather a splendid collection, actually," Parkinson said, stooping to inspect it. He had put a perfectly ordinary tan parka over a graph paper–checked ice cream–color suit.

There was a photographic portrait of King George VI in the uniform of Admiral of the Fleet. Parkinson and Pepper focussed on it intently. "Who did it, do you suppose?" they asked each other.

Parkinson bent lower, put his nose to the glass, stared fixedly in at the King, straightened himself up again. "The light in the eye has been retouched," he announced.

.    .    .

PARKINSON'S seventieth birthday came round. In the fashionable hired
rooms, photograph people bowed, squeaked, kissed the air at other photograph people, or sometimes cut them dead. I saw a man I know wearing
a look of bored alertness along with his dinner jacket, the way some of
the other men there wore cummerbunds. "Weddings, parties—there's
always something happening in this place," he said. "I'm often here.
Always the same guys, the same faces from the gossip column of *Women's
Wear.*"

"You're out a lot," I said.

"Every night, except when I'm in love."

Ann Getty (of the swans and peacocks) and Arianna Stassinopoulos,
the author and socialite, were giving the birthday party, and had invited
most of the guests. "Who is this Parkinson, anyway?" I heard people say.
Some months earlier, Parkinson had photographed Arianna Stassinopoulos in her native Greece, blithely waving scarves at the Parthenon
and then looking solemnly into the camera while wearing bunches of
grapes all over her head. ("We could have done the shot in the hotel
room," she told me later. "But he insisted on going into the vineyard and
picking the grapes himself. He said he wanted them with their—what's
that word?—*velvet* on.")

Around the white-robed tables in the dark green–painted room,
manners were hard to fault.

"Were you one of the group of ladies who went to the spa at Rancho
La Puerta?" asked the neighbor on my right.

The neighbor on my left, conversing in his turn, made a feather-light
allusion to having dined *en famille* with the Duke of Wellington. "My
wife's half my age, you know," he said next. Tortoiseshell-bespectacled,
and cozily buttoned into his double-breasted dinner jacket, he suggested

an expensively upholstered armchair. "My first wife and I were married for twenty-eight years. We came from the same world," he said, twisting in his seat and scanning the other tables for a glimpse of his present wife. The strangers making up the little circle at our table were lifting hands to mouths with clockwork motions, giving themselves judicious forkfuls and napkin dabs. "For the past ten years, I've had more darn fun," my neighbor said, turning back to his plate.

A woman with a Victorian coiffure said she was grateful for her piano, which enabled her to self-express. An elderly man with a completely naked head, sitting barely higher than the level of the place card ascribing to him a European barony, simply worked his jaws in silence, where he sat on her far side. The woman seated next to the baron seemed as far as he beyond both youth and small talk; she was peeping timidly out from her china-doll face colors while, on her bosom, a necklace of enormous rubies and diamonds gently rose and fell.

Dancing started, and rather more energetic table-hopping. Simon Parkinson and Terence Pepper were up and about, making much of the black shape, the whirr, the milky-green tongues of their Polaroids. A big birthday cake was carried in. It was topped with a chocolate version of Parkinson's famous embroidered smoking cap. (He always wears this while working, to fend off "gremlins," even when he is photographing queens; a regular supply is sent from Kashmir, where such hats are traditionally worn at weddings.) Parkinson put on the chocolate hat and rose from his seat between Geraldine Stutz, the president of Henri Bendel, and Suzy. Thanks to his two hostesses, he said (taking off the hat before it could melt), he had been able to gain access to the most exclusive, private sites in Germany and in Greece. He waved a piece of paper and craved his audience's indulgence while he read a telegram he had sent that day to Buckingham Palace. "Congratulations to Your Majesty on our birthday from her humble servant Norman Parkinson," he intoned. It seemed that it was the Queen's birthday, too.

Chairs were pushed back from the tables again. My married neighbor looked up eagerly as his wife—a striking blonde in a striking gown —passed by our table in a cloud of perfume and a rustle of silk. She headed for the table across the way, where a dark-haired man of her own age leaped to his feet and greeted her with a flurry of kisses. Her husband looked on. The pair were rubbing noses now; the younger man was waving his arms above his head like tree branches; they were wiggling their bodies at each other in samba movements. "They adore each other," the husband said, taking his eyes away and giving me a little nod. "But I don't have to—you know—*worry* about her with him."

"I think Parkinson finds most social life rather vapid," Wenda Parkinson once said to me. "And I'm really rather a recluse. When we're in London, we might go down to the corner pub for a glass of beer, and that's it. He has this obsession with agriculture, he really does. He can deliver cows and pigs—things like that. I seem to remember he won a plowing competition once. And he loves children. Our little grandson dotes on him."

The Parkinsons came back to their table after dancing to a ragged-sounding band of Greek musicians. Norman and Wenda Parkinson dance beautifully together under any circumstances.

"Did you think his speech went off all right?" Wenda Parkinson asked me, and smiled. "He is rather fun, isn't he?" Yes, today was his real birthday. "We had a tiny celebration at midnight last night, in our hotel room. He'd been out somewhere, as usual. I just put the little presents on the bed and said 'Happy Birthday, Old Thing.'"

My acquaintance from earlier in the evening was tilting on the back legs of his party-rental chair and contemplating across a table empty of all but flung-down napkins and uneaten desserts the sight of Carmen, the model, fox-trotting (in a different Vollbracht dress tonight) with one of the guest list's good-looking men. "This group feels *safe* here—at home," my acquaintance said. Jerome Zipkin, the man-about-town (he is the confidant of many wealthy women, including Nancy Reagan), was shepherding a posse of ladies in fashions as colorful as Caribbean postage stamps through the emptying tables to the door. "They dress up. They eat. They dance," my acquaintance said. He yawned, decisively tapped the tablecloth with two sets of fingertips, and made to rise. "The proverbial cruise to nowhere," he said.

NEXT night, I went down a sort of mirrored tunnel, a flight of red-carpeted stairs.

"Must be Chow's private room, the inner sanctum," came an alert, bored voice near my ear. "Not my usual turf," said my acquaintance, who was out again.

Martin Summers, a wealthy London gallery owner, had flown over his neighborhood youth orchestra for a concert to coincide with "Britain Salutes New York." ("We thought we ought to have a go," he said.) Now he was throwing a black-tie postconcert supper for a hundred and fifty people at the Mr. Chow restaurant. His wife, Nona—a slender woman in a long blue gown, with an animated manner and a Pre-Raphaelite mass of red hair—presided over a score or so of the guests who were to sit downstairs. Parkinson's head was immediately visible as I rounded the corner at the bottom of the stairs, and so was Carmen's electrified silvery coiffure. Steve Rubell, the former co-owner of Studio 54, was already seated at the long table, with his back to the upholstered wall. Another man was standing up with his back half turned to the door, extending his hand in greeting to each fellow-diner who came in. A sharply defined angle of his shoulder blades under well-tailored cloth lent him an air of almost adolescent vulnerability. "Calvin Klein," he was saying to one guest and then to the next, making a little, sketchy bow. Bianca Jagger, Mick Jagger's ex-wife and the mother of his daughter, stood at Klein's side, wearing a Velázquez-Infanta purple gown. "Calvin Klein," Calvin Klein said again, unfolding his napkin, as we all sat down. Platters of fashionable, pretty food were carried in and set down on the cloth between vases of narcissus and hyacinths. Calvin Klein picked up a platter and held it out for me to serve myself; Chow's dumplings shook slightly, in a little dance.

Parkinson had photographed Klein some days earlier. I asked Klein how it had gone.

"Wonderful," he said. "The best sitting I *ever* had. Mr. Parkinson is so funny, so kind, such a *gentleman.* " Tears welled up in his eyes. I looked up at the wall, at Steve Rubell, down at the flowers, at my plate, at Calvin Klein's. He had served himself a single bright-green snow pea and a single bright-pink shrimp. "I already ate, before I came," he said, recovering his poise.

Nona Summers had left her evening purse upstairs somewhere and was worrying about it. Suddenly, she was extricating herself from where she sat on the banquette and was climbing up onto the table and down the other side. Her feet in high-heeled blue satin slippers, her slim ankles in blue-spotted hose were there near eye level on the white cloth, next to the flowers and the snow peas, and then they were gone again.

Klein brought his face very close to mine. "I'm so tired," he said. "I've been working with thirty models all day, doing fittings for my collection. Working with women like that! You've no idea! They're *impossible!*"

Bianca Jagger leaned forward in her seat, on Calvin Klein's other side, and looked at him protectively. Klein moved his chair closer to mine and, picking up my hand from where it lay on the cloth, began to stroke it abstractedly as he went on talking in a conspiratorial tone.

Bianca Jagger leaned forward again and said she was ready to leave and go dancing.

"Anyone know someplace really sleazy?" Klein asked, pushing back his chair.

I turned to Parkinson and asked whether he had enjoyed his birthday party.

"A bit of the old puritan comes out in me sometimes," he said. "All those grapes and pineapples left over, just chucked in the dustbin. That *huge* cake, all that dessert. People hardly touched them—did you see?" He looked down the length of the table. "Café society," he said. "Doesn't faze me. New York doesn't faze me, either. But the Bowery isn't there for nothing, is it? It's as though there were success or failure here, and nothing in between." He'd spent his day giving interviews. "Reporters always ask the same eight questions," he said. " 'What's it like to work with the world's most beautiful women?' 'What's Koo Stark really like?' 'How do you get the Royals to relax?' Once, when I was having lunch with the Queen Mother, I said that we all appreciated how hard the Royal Family worked. Rather sycophantic, you might say. She said the hardest part of the job was all the chat. She said the terrible thing about walkabouts is that one asks something—'Have you been waiting long?' probably—and then moves on to the next group. But your words get passed down the line faster than you can move, and they haunt you all the way. And she said the worst part of all is when you get to the very end of the walkabout and people have been hanging about for four hours in the rain and when you speak to them the poor things just freeze up, out of exhaustion and nerves." Parkinson did an imitation of loyal subjects at the tail end of some drizzly British walkabout silently opening and shutting their mouths.

. . .

THE sky above Manhattan next morning was brilliant blue and dotted with
the little alligator-shaped white clouds of spring. I walked from my house
to buy a loaf of bread, passing a grizzled old man who sat on a stoop
waving a bottle of Night Train Express and talking to a group of garbage
cans. "I love my dog," he was saying. "I love my dog more than my
brother."

The store was a fancy one, selling bread that might be pink or green,
sometimes even striped. The two young men behind the counter had their
heads close together—in chefs' toques that were yeasty-looking and
cherry red—and were gossiping as if their lives depended on it.

"Then what did you do?"

"We ended up going over to Studio."

"Was it fun? Anyone there?"

"Calvin the K. was there, with Bianca. I always love to look at
Bianca."

CALVIN Klein's fashion show was surrounded by the usual swirl, the usual
struggle. Business people, press, and teams of buyers, from Europe,
Seventh Avenue, and Japan, frazzled by weariness and vanity, pushed at
each other in the shrunken space of his showroom's lobby, then broke
through at last to search, inside, for their names on long lines of seats
set up facing a runway. Camera wielders were strongest and boldest,
forging through with their knobby bags and leather straps and all the rest
of the impedimenta of the magic eye. A mirrored ceiling above the runway
reflected the progress of the twirling, stalking models in foreshortened
form and held the shifting patterns made by crowns of bright-colored hats.

Carrie Donovan, the fashion writer and senior editor of *The New York*

*Times Magazine,* pushed her huge spectacles back up her nose. "Will you *look* at that neck on Iman!" she said to André Leon Talley, the fashion writer, who was sitting with a hand on the silver handle of his umbrella.

The model Carmen sat in the audience with her chin resting lightly on fingers that looked carefully arranged, and watched the undulating progress of Iman with a professional appreciation. Jerry Hall's grand sunlit waterfall of waist-length blond hair swayed as she followed a few paces after Iman, wearing at the end of one slim arm a big shocking pink–dyed fox-fur muff. Her hand swung to and fro, the muff waving like a rhythmic censer at the knees of Jerome Zipkin, Bianca Jagger, Andy Warhol, and the striking blond wife, who were sitting in a line in the front row. Then Jerry Hall made her little dimpling smile—the lazy lift of the corners of her red-painted lips—and bestowed it like a posy of spring violets on Parkinson, who was sitting in the second row, wearing his striped suit and with a pin shaped like a teddy bear in his lapel.

PARKINSON'S head was tanned again when, one morning some weeks later, he looked out of the window of a car carrying him through Palm Beach. "Mrs. Vreeland always used to say, 'Remember, Parks, there is *nothing* more *unchic* than a *palm* tree. Don't let me *see* one in your pictures,' " Parkinson said, imitating the dramatic intonation of Diana Vreeland, the former editor-in-chief of American *Vogue.*

Nancy Tuck Gardiner, the beauty, health, and special-projects editor of *Town & Country,* was looking out of the window, too. Sprinklers swept surrounding lawns with rainbows. "That's the Merriweather Post house," she said. "Yoko Ono has bought a home here." Nancy Gardiner was a trim woman of thirty-eight with outstandingly good cheekbones and up-swept dark hair, who was dressed in a couture tracksuit. "There must be more grooming goes on in Palm Beach, more clipping removed per inch of yard, than anywhere else on earth," said Nancy Gardiner, who has lived in the resort for part of each year ever since she was born. "And we've got something like one policeman for every hundred people." This statistic makes for amicable relations: it had been arranged for an off-duty Palm Beach police officer to guard the jewelry to be used for several days of fashion shooting that Parkinson was embarking upon. At least, the local man would guard the half-million dollars' worth already on hand. "That nice man from Harry Winston" was scheduled to fly down from New York with the real biggies later that morning, Nancy Gardiner said.

Parkinson was wearing one of his specially made shirts—an Italian-silk number whose yellow-and-purple swirls had caused quite a reaction among the representatives of the National Beer Wholesalers' Association sitting at breakfast in the hotel dining room earlier. Except for the shirt, Parkinson looked more than ever like the empire builder setting off purposefully in morning sun at the head of a column of supply-laden bearers. "Wait till you see this museum," Parkinson said to me, of the Lannan Foundation, in Lake Worth, where part of the shoot was to take place. "It makes Picasso look like Millais."

"Wait till you see the Lannan house," Nancy Gardiner said, of the Palm Beach home of the magnate J. Patrick Lannan, where the rest of the shoot would take place. It seemed that museum and house were bulging with an enormous collection of modern art, which had been built up by Lannan, actively assisted in recent years by his friend the designer Mary McFadden. "Wait till you see what they did with this perfectly ordinary little house," Nancy Gardiner said. "At least, a perfectly ordinary little house with an ocean view and a lake view, which is worth five million right there."

The museum turned out to be a former movie theater, a Deco structure with white-painted buttresses sharply etched against the blue Florida sky. Beyond a set of heavy black doors, the lobby seemed ice-cold and dim. On a low clothes rack just inside the entrance of the museum (which was closed to the public that day) someone had hung a row of silky dresses in garnet, silver, ivory, and gold. They were shoulder to shoulder in the gloom, bent at the knees as if at prayer. Around them, gold-trimmed robes, ornamental belts, pharaonic bangles, peacock feathers, and stockings came spilling and tumbling out of opened trunks. In a brightly lit room off to one side, Iman was preparing to be photographed wearing some of these clothes (which were designed by Mary McFadden) by sitting with her Burmese-cat face tilted up toward Olivier Echaudemaison, a Parisian makeup artist whose living canvases have ranged in the past from Princess Anne (on her wedding day, and with the white fur and the tiara) to Josephine Baker (whose eyelids he adorned with spangles). Iman's husband, Spencer Haywood—one of the very few men whose legs can look cramped in the back of a Cadillac limousine—sat sprawled in white shorts in a nearby chair, and watched. "Even *I* only come up to his epiglottis," Parkinson had said of the former forward of the Washington Bullets. Parkinson had had an idea for a shot of the Haywoods in front of an electric-blue sculpture. (Unlike other shots planned for the coming session, this was not intended for an issue of *Town & Country* which would appear some months later.) The man was to be wearing a small, as yet unbought electric-blue swimsuit and to have his wife somehow riding on his hip "like an African woman's baby" and in an outfit as yet undisclosed. "I ain't going to be naked, Parks," Iman had said.

The museum's collection *was* amazing—a profusion of painting, ceramic, art glass, and other media, ranging from metal and wood to noise, neon light, and what looked like scraps of old soft-drink cans. The totemic, the talismanic, the mammoth. The hottest new art-world names alongside the well established. From high up in one corner of the gallery's main room—abutting some expansive squiggles by the young artist who moved from drawing all over the New York subway system to having annual sales exceeding a million dollars—a painting of a strange, crouching pea-green homunculus gazed down with a melancholy watermelon slice of a grin. Snaky coils of electric extension cords, stilt-legged crucibles of photographic lamps, and little families of aluminum camera valises contributed their share, this morning, to the museum's general homage to modern-art forms. Martin Seymour, Parkinson's American assistant—a young man with a ducktail haircut and a red T-shirt reading "AERO-MÉXICO GIVES WINGS TO YOUR DREAMS"—unpacked Parkinson's hat and threw it to him; Parkinson put it on. ("You must never just *pass* the hat to him," Parkinson's English assistant told me once. "The hats live in the camera bag, and you're responsible for them. Every year, there's a new hat to be trained to know everything the old hat knows.") The Hasselblad was set up on its tripod and pointed in the direction of a massive steel sculpture by Lucas Samaras, which Parkinson had designated on the previous day's reconnoitre as the background for the first of his fashion shots.

"It's supposed to be you having an *affair* with this thing," he had told Iman before she went to put on a McFadden dress and sequester herself with a hairdresser and the makeup man. Parkinson had settled down to wait. "It's always the same. An hour and a half to get the model ready, ten minutes for the shot," he said. The Samaras sculpture stood nearly as tall as Spencer Haywood. It was a gigantic, three-dimensional wrought-iron gate of a piece with heavy scrolls and barbed wire–style spikes, all made of thick rusted steel. "Iman will *fight* with this, just you see," Parkinson said. "Iman is *strong.*" Parkinson claims to have been the first photographer to work with Iman after she came from Somalia, at the outset of what has been a spectacular modelling career. She is known for the flexible, double-jointed quality of her slender chocolate-brown body, the length of neck supporting a tiny head, the expressive gestures of long-fingered hands. "She won't give those amazing fingers away to Bloomingdale's, you know," Parkinson said now. He demonstrated her famous articulated gestures, with some fingers winging up in exotic curves, others down. "She is very possessive of her fingers."

Across the room, under a tentlike hemp-and-metal piece by Barbara Chase Riboud, Nancy Gardiner was supervising her associate Robert Clark, who happens to be her nephew. ("Call me Bobo," he had told me when we were introduced the previous evening. "Everyone in the family does." The name is pronounced "Bobbo.") A dark-haired man of twenty-two with the worldly-wise manner and fuzzy waistline of one who has eaten many a meal with wealthy people twice his age, he was unpacking a box of jewelry from Cartier with a practiced hand—dipping a thumb and forefinger into little black pouches and fishing out sparkling bracelets and earrings. A slight man barely older than Clark but dressed in an ill-fitting vested suit with an old-fashioned wide necktie stood looking on with a most self-conscious air of responsibility: the man whom aunt and nephew had called "our policeman."

Parkinson was still waiting for Iman. "They command fantastic incomes, you know, these girls," he said. "It's like working with Elizabeth Taylor. Stars like Iman and Jerry gross two and a half million a year."

A gray-haired man standing nearby said that television crews were almost as expensive as models. He was David Burke, and he was producing a fifteen-minute segment on Parkinson for a magazine show that NBC was launching as its latest Sunday-evening assault wave against CBS and "Sixty Minutes." The competition had already broadcast a segment on the Earl of Lichfield, the Queen's cousin and one of the three main photographers trusted by the Royal Family, the others being the Earl of Snowdon and Parkinson. Lichfield had been promoting his new collection of designer luggage when he appeared on "Sixty Minutes." He is also known for advertisements in which fellow-aristocrats wear Burberry raincoats, and for an automobile-parts company's annual calendar in which young women wear almost no clothes at all. Burke's crew consisted of a cameraman and a soundman—two energetic men in their thirties, both with curly hair and mettlesome suntans acquired during past days in Florida. They were bustling about the museum, setting up the equipment with which they would record images of Parkinson recording his images. Alongside their elaborate video equipment, Parkinson's camera—on its tripod, with an opened, light-directing white parasol over it and a humble plastic shopping bag with extra lenses dangling underneath—looked antediluvian, something out of a boardwalk scene by William Merritt Chase. The three television men had last worked as a team on a documentary about some Marxist revolutionaries on what had been at the time the completely obscure Caribbean island of Grenada. Now they had been following Parkinson and his fashion-shoot entourage (which included the models Jerry Hall, Apollonia van Ravenstein, and Carmen as well as Iman) for several days. "You should have seen Apples walking around the hotel at Bonaventure in these incredible black-and-white striped tights," one of the television men said.

Iman came out of the dressing room. She was wearing a clinging black column of silky stuff with a ruffle at the hem. ("We can make her look like a *razor blade*," Parkinson had said as he supervised Seymour's placing of powerful photographic lights.) Her hair was folded close to her small head, and a tremendous foot-and-a-half-high crest of black feathers had been pinned in an arc from the back of her head to her brow, in the style of a kingfisher's crest. She walked over to the sculpture, in high-heeled shoes. A short man with a blue shirt and a proprietary expression came trotting behind, preening the feathers with the long, spiked tail of a comb. This was René Romeu, who had flown in for the shoot. ("He is the chic-est, poshest hairdresser in New York," Parkinson had told me firmly. "He works in the Pierre in a terribly *private* way, with people like

Mrs. Gordon Getty or Arianna Stassinopoulos.") Parkinson stood behind his camera and talked Iman into position. Her back was against the sculpture, with its curls and axelike blades of rusting steel.

"Knee up, darling. . . . Fingers like spikes. Very *spiky,* chicken. . . . Shoulders back. Head down. We don't want to lose an inch of that neck. . . . You haven't got your swept back right! I want to see that black ass! . . . Stay, baby."

The powerful muscle at the side of her neck slanted like the rope that raises a drawbridge. Her back, between shoulders and buttocks, curved inward in an astonishing parabola. Between the camera's whirrs and clicks, Romeu and Echaudemaison darted crouchingly up to her, made slight adjustments, and fell back again.

"We'll now get this right!" Parkinson said. "One wrist higher than the other. Fingers up!" He was almost bellowing now. "Spikes! More spikes!"

"These shoes are killing me," Iman said.

THE heavy black doors to the outside world opened wide enough to admit a pie wedge of blinding, humid air, and also Spencer Haywood, returning from a trip to a sporting-goods store with Parkinson's son, Simon, who had flown up from Trinidad for the duration of the shoot. After all, hadn't Nancy Gardiner described the events as "a bit of history being made"? Haywood was wearing mirrored sunglasses and carrying in one huge hand (its fingers, each with one more knuckle than on a normal hand, are almost as prehensile as Iman's) a small scrap of electric blue.

"He's going to need some baby oil," Olivier Echaudemaison said.

The black doors opened again, admitting another strip of damp whiteness, and also the rumbling and admonitory peep-peeping sounds of a dump truck doing road work in the street. Jerry Hall, stepping out of a black limousine with her butter-colored hair bouncing in recently hot-rollered ringlets, had to cross a baking strip of soft sand where the sidewalk had been, earlier that morning.

"Why, hello, y'all," she said to the company as she came in. She smiled. Before Jerry Hall's first shot and the African-baby tableau, there was to be a double head-shot of the Haywoods (for Spencer's modelling portfolio, someone said) and more time to kill.

"Don't comb Jerry's hair out yet, René," Parkinson said, sitting down under a towering structure that looked like a Maori totem pole.

"Of course, I feel an aesthetic responsibility to the museum and the artists," he said, turning to me. "I know these chaps are the real thing. We are only the second eleven—the recorders and the copyists, not the originals." He waved at a nearby canvas that he wanted to use as a background for Haywood seeming to hold his wife's head "like a nut" and as if floating in his big hands. "I feel very privileged to have the opportunity to work with an early Kenneth Noland *Target,*" he said. He launched into a rambling allegory about two people, a plate of Brown Windsor soup, and a stain that even Lilliman & Cox, the Mayfair dry cleaners, couldn't get out. "That's what fashion's all about," he said at the end.

IN THE dressing room, Iman was expressing reservations about heavy black pencil marks that Echaudemaison had added to her husband's eyebrows, which made him look like the Moor of Venice waiting for his cue. Echaudemaison handed Haywood a brush and told him to brush his beard, and then turned his attention to the upturned face of the wife. Romeu was holding a little switch of black hair and thoughtfully swishing it into the palm of one hand. He proffered the root end to me, and I grasped it in my fist while he used both his hands to comb it with rapid tugging movements, mold it, and cover it with a fine-mesh net.

"Sculptural," Iman said, looking intently at the shape of her mouth in a mirror and pausing with a loaded lip brush in her hand. "It's got to be sculptural."

Romeu pinned the hairpiece like a little black question mark on the very top of her head.

"That ain't sculptural," she said, and he unpinned it and started all over again.

Simon Parkinson sat on a half-landing aiming an electric fan at Jerry Hall, who had put on a black-and-white evening gown. The fabric of its skirt molded her legs on one side, blew ripplingly away from them on the other.

"Open the mouth, darling!" called Parkinson *père,* from under his reflecting parasol. He kept quickly turning the handle to roll the film on, and it went *clicketa-whirr, clicketa-whirr.* "Swing your hair! Swing your hair!"

She twisted her waist, flung up her arms, and, by flipping her head back and forth, made for his lens (as she had done in Russia and in Marie Antoinette's boudoir in past years) a flying-halo effect with her long gold hair. Emerging, trophylike, from the wall just above her, a faceless, helmeted black figure by the artist Robert Longo reached down toward the shining hair with widespread arms, as if it wanted to embrace her. Sapphires and diamonds sparkled at her fingers and her ears. Martin Seymour stepped forward, chewing gum, and held the black box of his light meter up to her powdered cheek. The television camera sat like a big black monkey on the shoulder of the curly-headed cameraman. Simon Parkinson swivelled his fan. The skirt was blowing out, and a Calder mobile was spinning like a carousel.

"René!" Parkinson shouted. "Where are you? We need you to help the hair!"

Over and over, the hair flew out. Over and over, the figure made its sinuous movements like a jumping summer-evening fish. On the wall above the Longo man was an artist's version of the Stars and Stripes, overlaid, as with a graven image, by a baleful-looking gold-colored calf.

THE members of the NBC crew were assessing their morning's take by replaying their videotape. They pressed a fast-forward button, and scenes from the immediate past were replayed at lunatic speed on the four-inch screen of their portable recorder, which was sitting on the floor. Voices came out of the little black box in speedy, mouselike squeaks. Then the men pressed another button, and the image was frozen at a single frame.

"That's great," Iman said. "Now we can know exactly when we got the shot."

At normal speed, here was the sequence of Parkinson photographing the Haywoods in front of the Noland *Target*. There was a pint-size Parkinson, a parasol small enough for a Polynesian cocktail, two tiny black heads framed by concentric halos of red and green paint.

"Like a nut!" said Parkinson's voice, from the black box.

"Little white teeth!" the voice said authoritatively.

Parkinson had strolled across the museum and stood with folded arms gazing down at the scaled-down version of himself. He looked at once dismissive and amused. "Funny old man," he said, with a smile. "Why do I always sound like Prince Philip?"

Echaudemaison appeared with a bottle of baby oil in his hand and waved it in the direction of the life-size Spencer Haywood, who was horizontally extended—at what seemed like infinite length—prone on the rug by Parkinson's feet, his nose at the level of the miniature image of himself and his wife being photographed. He started doing pushups in preparation for his next appearance.

"Got to pump 'em up a bit," he said, getting back on his feet and ambling off with the makeup man.

THE black doors opened again, and suddenly the tone of the gathering was changed, the museum charged by the presence of a handful of solid-looking men wearing tan suits, dark glasses, and "Magnum, P.I." mustaches, and giving the impression that their beefy hands were hovering over hidden guns. A white-haired man, looking distinctly damp and rumpled from his journey, put down a briefcase near the totem pole, opened it, and took out some manila envelopes. "That nice man from Harry Winston" had arrived, with his security guards and his two million dollars' worth of diamonds.

"We'll give Jerry a nice big rock to play with," someone said. "That'll keep her happy."

The Harry Winston man was methodically licking his thumb and using it to separate and set out sheets of clean white tissue paper, which became bedding for a succession of sparkling bracelets, necklaces, earrings, rings.

In the passage between the dressing room and the main gallery hung a canvas by the painter Julian Schnabel, a bright-yellow work adorned with paint-smeared pieces of what looked like jungle-animal hide. ("I think Mr. Lannan would have preferred one of Schnabel's broken-pot canvases," the museum's curator, Nancy Mato, had told me. "But I think this is a little *different.* ") In front of the brown-and-yellow painting, the giant figure of Spencer Haywood now hove into view, his muscular black body gleaming all over with a coat of baby oil and clad only in the smallest of electric-blue swimsuits. Echaudemaison followed, with two bright spots in his cheeks. The man from Harry Winston looked up from his unpacking and stopped stock-still—a freeze frame of himself with a freshly licked thumb held up and cooling in the air. The tan suits shifted about and gave each other significant glances from behind their dark glasses.

Parkinson, Seymour, Echaudemaison, Haywood, and Iman—with a length of blue fabric covering her head and her person, and stepping on high-arched bare feet, like an African madonna—formed a loose procession, mounted some stairs, and disappeared from view on the balcony, where the electric-blue sculpture was installed. The Winston man finished setting out the row of diamonds. They were dazzling, abundant, accessible. It seemed, as I stood near them, that there was something violent about their beauty.

Jerry Hall, dressed in a brief cloth-of-gold tunic, and with her hair rearranged to tumble over brows that were bound in a gold-braid headband like that of a Wagnerian Brünnhilde, came skipping out of the dressing room and made a beeline for the diamonds laid out under the totem pole. She tried on earrings, held bracelets to her wrist, slipped onto her finger a ring with a stone as big as one of the exotic eggs at Le Cirque, and turned her hand this way and that to see the flashes of refracted light.

"*She's* not shy," said the voice that had spoken earlier.

From the unseen balcony upstairs we could hear the *clicketa-whirr* of Parkinson's camera and repeated echoing thumps of someone's bare feet landing hard on the carpeted floor. "One, two, three, go!" Parkinson could be heard to bellow between the *clicketa-whirrs* and thumps. "Go! Go!"

The young policeman in charge of the half-million dollars' worth of Cartier jewels was visibly more relaxed in view of the more powerful showing of the Winston diamonds and their security team. He was chatting with the NBC crew about the Lannan house, to which the caravan was scheduled to move for further poses, among the sculpture-filled grounds. "They got art all over the yard," the policeman was saying. "At least, they call it art. I call it rocks."

"Lift her up! Lift her up!" the Prince Philip voice was heard to boom from the balcony. "Hand on her bum!"


EVEN the front door of the Lannan house was like a piece of sculpture. Mary McFadden put her head around it and invited me to step in. The designer, who is renowned in fashion circles for an appearance almost as stylized as Diana Vreeland's, had a cap of very straight, very fine, very black hair parted at the center and cut in a mathematical-looking bob. Normally, this frames a complexion of cultivated pallor, but Mary McFadden's face was on this occasion tinged with pink, from her having played three hours of tennis with a Palm Beach pro. After these exertions, she had dressed in her present costume of calf-length floating purple skirt; long, duster-style coat striped in yellow, turquoise, peach, and green; and bronze leather Capezios—the kind with little heels. We went out to a terrace and looked down a hundred feet of garden to the edge of Lake Worth. There was a swimming pool, a blaze of geraniums, a waft of gardenia, a little lizard rustling under a fallen leaf. And there was art: art like rocks, or flying tents, or piles of railway ties, or heavy engineering.

"This is by Isamu Noguchi," Mary McFadden said, laying a palm flat against a large rounded bronze. "We happen to think he is the most important living sculptor." The view was dominated by a metal X shape —white-painted, as big as a house, and rising out of green lawn to punctuate the blue of sky and lake beyond. "That's by Ronald Bladen," she said. "We have over two thousand art works on three acres here."

Inside the house, the rooms were cool and dim, striped with thin slits of light from louvered shutters. "This is a Chia, a new acquisition," she said, gesturing with a hand at the end of its multicolored sleeve. Her bronze leather shoes went tapping through the corridors and rooms. "This is a work in ceramic, gold leaf, and feathers. This is a little Picasso. This is by an artist working conceptually in punctuated newspaper. These are two Brice Mardens, this is the Giacometti room. This is some pre-Columbian stuff; some Egyptian; this is another Chia; this is by a Yugoslavian artist unheard of in the West; this is one Conceptual artist's idea of a teapot." We were passing through a bedroom with a disordered, unmade bed. "The sheets are from my Crystal Dreams collection for Martex," Mary McFadden said, with a quick laugh. The unidentified sleeper must have wakened under the gaze of a pair of strange, sad, lumpen, gaily colored figures that were as compelling as the crouching pea-green homunculus in the painting back at the museum, and were clearly by the same hand. "George McNeil," Mary McFadden said, looking up at the two big canvases and giving a little nod. "We were one of the first collectors to rediscover him. He's in his seventies now. He's been painting all his life, but he was kind of ignored for a lot of his career. Now, with the return of the figurative, things are changing for him. He worked on this one canvas for years and years." She brought her birdlike head and eye right up against the canvas and looked at it. "Perhaps it is just a *little* overworked."

We passed through a windowless hall. "From the tombs of the dead in Madagascar," she said, waving at some carved pieces. "I used to have a much larger collection." She touched a switch; lights and the music of a Solemn Mass sprang up. "Frederick Kiesler's chapel," she said. "When it was shown at the Musée Rodin and the Whitney, it had black velvet on the walls."

We passed through a door into the garden. A bird was singing. To one side of the path was a huge round stone with a hole in it, like a giant Lifesaver, upright on a stand. "That's what they used for money on the island of Yap," Mary McFadden said. "Just the way in China you measure wealth by the number of ducks in your back yard." We went through another door and into a separate, private gallery, filled with yet more art. A huge curved form in hammered, gilded metal was gleaming from the center of the place; it hung suspended, as if by magic, from invisible wires. "A Mark di Suvero, from his Park Place period," my guide said. "And over here is an early Clifford Still." Next to it was a canvas with two pairs of disembodied legs locked in a swastika shape, tumbling through space. "Another Yugoslavian artist," Mary McFadden said. "Unfortunately, his work got a little crazy. He started painting rats eating fetuses."

THE sound of crunching gravel, like breaking waves, came from the direction of the driveway, and there was a chorussed thudding of car doors. Parkinson and the fashion shoot had come on from the Lannan Foundation. The NBC crewmen unloaded their equipment from their hired truck and headed for sandwiches that had been set out on a table on the porch. Echaudemaison unzipped his cases, which were filled with row after row of brushes with soft, blush-tinted ends, and laid them on the table alongside the food. Apollonia van Ravenstein, who had been free to spend the earlier part of the day by the hotel pool, was deftly rolling up her long auburn hair on heated rollers. She was dressed in a slinky white McFadden gown, ready for her first scheduled pose: perching alongside Iman (in another white gown) and Jerry Hall (in white and black) on top of some white marble blocks on a lawn. Above the silky stuff, her bare back looked fiery pink from the morning's sun. Martin Seymour was summoned and started gently rubbing it with cream. The NBC team, shifting from one sneakered foot to the other and taking great half-moon bites out of sandwiches, nudged each other and agreed that they would have been happy to land that particular job. Iman was sitting with her face tilted up while Echaudemaison and Mary McFadden stood over her, looking down.

"You are more beautiful than ever," Mary McFadden said to Iman. "I was so worried when I heard about your taxicab accident. But when I saw that photograph of you in last Friday's *Women's Wear* I said 'Thank God!' "

Iman said that she had been flung right through the partition, that the damage to her face had been horrible, that they had had to wire her jaw.

Someone mentioned one of the beautiful women who had been at Summers' dinner at Mr. Chow; after *her* accident and the plastic surgery, the group agreed, she had never looked quite the same.

Iman's eyes as they looked upward to where Mary McFadden stood were deep-brown, twinkling, and set at the center of exaggerated, catlike frames of eyeshadow. Echaudemaison took up his sable brush and paid tribute to Iman's cheekbones with a bevy of reassuring flicks.

THE party straggled outside and around the end of the house to the vivid-green lawn where Parkinson's camera had been set up facing the group of large white marble blocks. The NBC camera had been set up facing Parkinson's. A palm tree stood nearby, its trunk at a slant against a sky that suddenly looked troubled, and its fronds having unchicly turned their undersides up in a stiffening breeze. Romeu was carrying a long auburn horsetail of extra hair and humming to himself as he swished it against his trouser leg. Joseph Stashkevetch, a young man with a solemn expression under a flat-topped crewcut, had been assigned by the McFadden company as a stylist for the shoot, but so far there hadn't seemed much of anything for him to do. ("Parks doesn't need a stylist," someone had said.) It was Nancy Gardiner who was busily improvising a pair of Grecian-style sandals out of a couple of lengths of gold string. Joseph Stashkevetch wandered by, all prepared with a pair of spare pantyhose that someone just might need; the calves and feet came dangling out of the pocket of his baggy shorts like the calves and feet of a ghost. Iman was showing Mary McFadden the Polaroids of herself and the electric-blue swimsuit; Mary McFadden looked shocked. The NBC crew was standing about nearby. "These are not for you," Iman said, with a toss of her head at the men, and she folded the photographs to her chest.

She climbed into position on a four-foot-high block of marble, with her hands raised Indian-goddess style in the air. Apollonia van Ravenstein half reclined on a six-foot-high block. Jerry Hall and her hair were spread out on the two-foot-high block between them. Her knee formed a sharp right angle where it was crooked up under the long silk skirt.

Martin Seymour half shaded his eyes with a flat hand and looked up at the approaching clouds. "You've got about three minutes of sun left, Parks," he said.

"Powder her feet, someone! Powder her feet!" Parkinson said. "I know it's hot on that rock, but try to relax the face."

"One minute, Parks."

*Clicketa-whirr, clicketa-whirr.* Faster and faster.

"This is a classic," Nancy Gardiner said.

*Clicketa-whirr, clicketa-whirr.* You could hear the ocean, on the other side of the road—unseen from where we stood. The approaching curtain of pewter-colored storm cloud was lighter gray near the edges, then bordered with sun-gilded lace.

"Thirty seconds, Parks."

He snapped on and on.

Jerry Hall and the Haywoods were flying back to New York in a couple of hours. "I'm losing all my *stars,*" Parkinson had moaned when he was informed.

The light was switched off, abruptly, in the sky. Everything went very quiet.

Jerry Hall sat upright on her rock and, lifting both hands to her nape, flipped out her hair. "Did you git it, Parks?" she said, with a plaintive note in her Texas voice. "You git the shot?"

Parkinson snapped the legs of his tripod shut decisively, turned on his heel, and strode away across the lawn toward the private gallery. "We'll do one last shot for the day, inside," he said. I hurried to keep pace with him as he rounded the pool and the art that looked like a flying tent. "I never believed in using that one black-and-white dress," he muttered, looking grim. We were passing the money from the island of Yap. "How could anyone possibly *live* with women like that?" he asked.

WHICH of the art works might qualify for the last-minute, unplanned triple shot? This one? That? The Mark di Suvero, of course! Bobo Clark leaped into action, dusted off the floor in front with a piece of rag. Parkinson would pose his beauties here, their complexions warmed by the luster of the sculpture, which was shaped like a giant pelvic bone and made of brass dipped in gold. He arranged the three women in harmonies: white dresses, a white hand and a black hand together, mingled tresses of gold and copper, this head in another's lap. All the ingredients were interwoven; he was using the utmost tact.

"It's almost a David," Nancy Gardiner said. "The harem, you remember?"

"Ingres," Parkinson said firmly. "That famous seraglio." His face looked tired and pleased. His cheeks and the top of his bald head were marked with big red lipstick kisses where the three models, converging, had congratulated him.

"Ingres," Nancy Gardiner said. "Exactly."

. . .

"I've wasted most of my life running after women or running away from them," Jim Kimberly said cheerfully at dinner that night. He was a sinewy, suntanned, soft-voiced man with white hair—a couple of years older than Parkinson, who was his guest of honor. Kimberly—whose grandfather co-founded the timber-and-paper company that became Kimberly-Clark, makers of Kleenex—was wearing a red mess jacket and a black silk ascot, and had a little gold earring in one ear. He was looking remarkably cheerful, in fact, for a man who loves women and who, having invited Iman, Jerry Hall, Apollonia van Ravenstein, and Carmen to a twelve-course banquet in a private room at the Breakers hotel, had been joined instead by René Romeu, Olivier Echaudemaison, Martin Seymour, Bobo Clark, Simon Parkinson, and the men from NBC. (Nancy Gardiner was also there, as socially spry as ever, though she had been up since four.) After the doors had closed behind a humble and grateful society-page photographer from the Palm Beach *Daily News,* the banquet began, with the claws of stone crabs. Kimberly explained how men fish the crabs out, pull off a spiny claw, then throw them back again to grow another. Course followed upon course. There were fingerbowls, a half-time sherbet, some very important wines. Kimberly talked of his days as a racing driver, with Fangio and Portago—all the greats.

"I used to race Alfa Romeos myself," said Parkinson, setting down his glass.

("Well, perhaps he *did* do a rally or two," his son said later. "He certainly had some very fast cars.")

The talk got round to the Reagans. It was agreed that Nancy Reagan wrote very nice little thank-you notes.

"I have known him since he was an announcer in Iowa," Kimberly said of the President, in his quiet voice.

"What's that you say? Since he was a Nazi?" Parkinson said.

Echaudemaison was sitting next to Kimberly's wife, Jacquie—a woman who is her husband's junior by several decades and whose pastimes include free-falling out of airplanes. Echaudemaison picked up her cigarette pack from the tablecloth, shook out a cigarette for her, then lit it, using her gold lighter. Parkinson got on his legs and told some anecdotes.

At that time, a photograph of Prince Andrew's girlfriend Koo Stark could be worth thousands of pounds on Fleet Street or to a European paparazzo. She was registered at the hotel with the rest of our party, but under a different name. "She's an American girl," Nancy Gardiner had said sympathetically. "She's used to being free." I shared a ride over to the following morning's shoot with Koo Stark and her mother, a sandy-haired American woman dressed in country-club style with sensible sandals and a white cotton golfing visor. Koo Stark was chatting about England and America in a lisping English accent. Which nationality was her father, then, I asked. She turned her head abruptly away from me and made a little strangled sound.

Parkinson crooked his finger at me on the porch of the Lannan house a bit later, and took me aside. "You are not allowed to ask her any direct questions without the permission of a certain gentleman in London," he said. He moved across to where Koo Stark was sitting on a sofa and, sitting down next to her, circled her with an arm. "This is the daughter I never had," I heard him say.

Her mother, who sat nearby flipping through the pages of a magazine, looked over the top of her spectacles at the pair, as if surprised.

·   ·   ·

SIMON Parkinson continued to pile up Polaroids for a private album of his own. Echaudemaison and Clark had also taken to firing away at the group. Someone was always lifting the unwieldy black box of a Polaroid camera to his eye, triggering off the cicada whine of the emerging print.

"I got these million-dollar babies with no makeup, with their Walkmen on their heads," Simon Parkinson said. "They've got to know they can trust you if they let you do that."

There were the elder Parkinson's professional Polaroids of each fashion pose as well. Nancy Gardiner was sticking them in a school-exercise book and writing the title of each Lannan art work in her rounded, schoolgirl hand. There was Iman with yesterday's steelwork—how long ago it seemed! The Longo man, the marble classic, the seraglio were there, and others as well—Mary McFadden in Mary McFadden, and Jerry Hall in the Brünnhilde headband, with the great big diamond between her teeth.

This morning's Polaroid of Apollonia van Ravenstein, on one leg and perched high up in the sky on top of Ronald Bladen's X, was a distillation of two sweltering hours of fetching ladders, watching clouds, and cajoling a reluctant hairdresser who turned out to be afraid of heights. Participants in and witnesses of the shot looked at the Polaroid with a passionate curiosity.

"There's the shot we need to get," the NBC men said. "A closeup of the Polaroid being held by a woman's hand."


THE entire caravan moved back to the museum. Now even the security guards joined the group watching each instant replay on the tiny video screen. It had become the moment that linked us: the hearth, the icon, the key.

"We're all such narcissists," Parkinson said, looking down at his small double yet again. He listened to his own patter as he had photo-graphed Apollonia van Ravenstein on the **X**—the jokes, the bursts of French-speaking and song. "Funny old man," he said again.

Carmen had got really sunburned the day before, beside the hotel pool. She was wearing a thick layer of makeup and trying not to move her face. Nancy Gardiner wanted her as a Silver Beauty at the center of a piece that was a wildly exploding mass of tangled silvery wire. Bobo Clark borrowed a utility knife from Martin Seymour and cut open a fresh cardboard carton of jewels. Eight hundred and sixty thousand dollars' worth, the invoice said.

"Bobo?" Nancy Gardiner called as he busied himself with little black pouches again.

"Yes, darling?"

"Any of it any good?"

"I think so," he said.


PARKINSON was jumpily protective of his first session with Koo Stark. The NBC crew had gone out to lunch when she left the seclusion of the dressing room. Romeu had been busy teasing her long hair into dense, fluffy peaks that fell straight downward for the moment, completely veil-ing her face. As she crossed behind the Chase Riboud, walking with a funny, stiff little glide (as of one who has known finishing schools, and books on the head), she looked like a palm tree on the move.

"She's never going to be able to hold that serious look," her mother said. Parkinson had set up the young woman with her chin resting on a stand that held a marquise-cut, kite-shaped piece of sparkling crystal. It was as big as her head, and her face was half hidden behind it. The hair now streamed outward and off the small, elaborately made-up face. A diamond diadem marked the hairline of the enormously aerated halo;

shafts of light streamed diagonally through the hair and the crystal from a powerful lamp Seymour had set up behind her.

"Lift the eyebrow, darling. Part the lips."

The single eye that had a clear line of sight to Parkinson and his camera stared back at them with a look of absolute trust.

"He took her on the top of the Trump Tower, with the whole of New York at her feet, and her dress blowing out to here in the wind," her mother said. "He told her not to look down."

"More serious, darling," Parkinson was murmuring, lifting his head from his camera and looking at her. *"Comme une odalisque."*

Nancy Gardiner was resting under the totem pole, across the room. "Parks wanted a very *young* look for Koo," she said. "A sort of bookend for the layout, along with Carmen. Youth and Age." She told me she had first worked with Parkinson in 1976. "Then we needed some big beauty heads," she said. "We used very young girls, and did it off a theming of Victorian nudes. A man had just published a great book on the subject. Oh, what was his name? The one who committed suicide."


ON THE other side of the big black doors, it was small-town, nineteen-forties America, and it was really, really hot. The dump truck was rumbling and peep-peeping away in the distance at the far end of the street, but there was no other sign of life. The storefronts of the cinder-block buildings seemed achingly white against the blue of the afternoon sky. The scalloped canvas awning of Dawn's News & Smoke, the barber pole outside Smokey's left shadows on the sidewalk as sharp as arty photographic prints. I found Bobo Clark standing with an elbow resting on the serving hatch of a sandwich hut that stood at the very center of a parking lot. He was perspiring as he placed a complicated multiple order for tuna and pastrami submarines. He loved working on these shoots, he said as he sat down to wait for the sandwiches, but he was tired. "There was the whole thing at Bonaventure last weekend, and a ceremony for Parkinson in the Sky Club at Pan Am before we left New York. And I was doing a whole lot of crazy running around with Murray in the limousine for months before that. I know how to handle problems on shoots—select the jewelry, make sure the girls are happy. But I feel I could do *more*. That's why I've started working with Nikki Haskell. We went to Brazil together and spent time with Ivo Pitanguy—you know, the famous plastic surgeon? He has this theory of the inner person and the outer person. It's a whole philosophy with him. Oh, there are so many things I could do. I'm very creative." The young man's gaze roamed outward, over the tops of the parked cars. A very old man appeared just then—a frail figure framed by the space between two rows of cars. He wore a white cap with a pom-pom on top; calf-high black socks; and knee-length shorts of check-patterned green polyester, held up by a white plastic belt. He was moving very cautiously, and leaning on a cane.

"I NOTICED there was a man upstairs all made out of wood chips," Apollonia van Ravenstein had said at the Lannan Foundation. "Couldn't we do a shot with him, Parks? I could have my arms round his neck. I could be *strangling* him!"

"I need a big beauty head," Nancy Gardiner had said, drawing the line at strangling. The model was sitting meekly in a low-necked gown while Echaudemaison supported one of her hands in his and rapidly brushed each of her nails in turn with a coat of colored polish.

The wood-chip man was the least mysterious of the objects on the second-floor balcony space. I touched a switch beside a sheet of steel that had strips curling out of it like the tongues of dragons; the thing flexed and shook itself with a thunderous rattling sound. I stepped to the edge of the balcony and looked over. No one seemed to have been disturbed by the noise. Parkinson stood feeling his mustache and pondering a background for Carmen's next shot; I could see the embroideries on top of his hat.

"With the long shots and the outdoor stuff, we've got just about everything our story needs, except the interview," David Burke had said to me that morning. Joseph Stashkevetch, shoeless and wearing pale-pink socks ("Rowed for Westminster, did you?" Simon Parkinson had asked him jovially, referring to his own and his father's old school), was beginning to fold up the McFadden dresses and stow the peacock feathers back in the travelling trunks. The pea-green homunculus continued to grin from the wall. I found a crude, white-painted wooden box with a little label reading "Galactascope," and a switch, which I clicked on and off a couple of times. I looked over the balcony and saw David Burke appear from the direction of the dressing room, flanked by his crew. He was wearing a violet silk McFadden tunic over his slacks and shoes. His face was framed by the Brünnhilde headband and a pair of jewelled hoop earrings, and looked as solemn as an Indian bridegroom's. He stood beside the totem pole, his arms straight down by his sides. The curly-haired men skipped round him with excited cries.

"The wire! Let's get a shot of him in that silver wire!"

"We're going to need another extension cord!"

David Burke closed his eyes. "I could really get into this," he said.

The Galactascope was working after all. A pale projected image of the planet Earth had appeared on the wall of the room, high up. The translucent green globe, delicately marbled with its continents and seas, sat quivering where it had crept into an empty space between the works of art.

• • •

PRINCE Andrew and Koo Stark took up photography quite intensively in the succeeding months, then gave up each other. Parkinson advised them. The Prince's snaps of his gamekeeper and of a sentry in his busby seen from an upper window at Windsor Castle appeared, together with Koo Stark's photographs of the paparazzi photographing her, in an exhibition called "Personal Points of View." His Royal Highness persuaded Parkinson to postpone an engagement in Texas and fly to London for the opening. That was a ruse to maneuver Parkinson into being the subject of Britain's high-rated television program "This Is Your Life." Koo Stark married the youthful heir to a trading-stamp fortune. Calvin Klein gave an interview to *Women's Wear Daily* to refute widespread rumors that he was a dying man. His portrait by Parkinson came out, and it was a tender one, with a cat in it. J. Patrick Lannan died, leaving his collections in trust to the Lannan Foundation and its trustees, including Mary McFadden. The NBC crew had gone down to Tobago and done a few more days of shooting; their segment was scheduled for one Sunday evening, but nobody in New York ever saw it, because the N.F.L. game ran into extra time. Apollonia van Ravenstein married and announced her retirement. Jerry Hall gave birth to Mick Jagger's daughter. Parkinson was mad keen to get some exclusive snaps of the child, with all its bloom. He whirled along with a thousand new commissions anyway. He photographed Isabella Rossellini and the Queen of Jordan, and a number of naked young women (these last for the calendar of the Pirelli tire company; this photographic project was also recorded by a documentary-film crew). He set off for Tokyo, where a big show of his work was mounted at the museum of the Isetan department store. He came away from Japan with film of yet another fashion shoot and with lots of new anecdotes, including one about a fashionable woman who most particularly wanted him to meet her parrot.

# AS GORGEOUS
# AS IT GETS

---

*I wanted a new fragrance, so I started mixing the finest oils and essences. I worked on one, and that came out lovely. I worked on another, and that came out lovely. I put them together and that came out beautiful.*

—Estée Lauder on the making of her new scent, Beautiful

A\WAY with those blue-and-white boxes! Mrs. Lauder wanted pink. Just as the new scent, Beautiful, was to be unveiled before several hundred eager employees at her company's sales meeting in May of 1985, Estée Lauder had had one of her legendary intuitions, and now the packaging was to be changed to a bright pink.

"Don't say hot pink or shocking pink," her public-relations staff instructed me. "We consider those incorrect. This is Mrs. Lauder's personal choice of an audacious pink. This is Beautiful Pink."

Even as the field executives were flying in from all over the country to the three-day session at the Woodcliff Lake Hilton, in Woodcliff Lake, New Jersey, a shell-shocked inner circle was rallying to produce new samples—not only of boxes but of a host of matching sales accessories to pep up store counters at the time of the scent's September debut. For most of the sales meeting's three hundred–odd participants —mainly women, well coiffed, well painted, and very ladylike in their style of dress—the bombshell brought only the slightest shift in the schedule of their seminars. "The New Heroine," the theme, or "color story," of Estée Lauder's new cosmetic promotion for the forthcoming fall was nudged forward; the blushing new Beautiful remained behind closed doors while last-minute transformations were carried out. As unperturbed and placid as some dowager, the "Christmas '85 luncheon" went right on waiting in a ruby-lit ballroom down the hallway, its silent tables all decked out with frosty twigs and shining balls.

"There's a lot of India in the air this year," June Leaman told a group assembled in one of the conference rooms to learn all about the latest color story. "And something country. But not rugged country. Country squire. Country estates. *Rich* country." She was a blonde in her fifties, a shade heavyset, perhaps, and with a manner at once warm and tough. She has one of the biggest jobs—senior vice-president, corporate creative marketing—in a billion-dollar corporation, and her womanly person bespoke, somehow, bulldog battles and pipers paid. "There are heroines all around us," she said. "Prime ministers. Astronauts. Every one of us here leads a heroine's life." She produced a poster of Willow Bay, a young model, photographed on the streets of London wearing a fair amount of makeup and carrying a pair of bright-red gloves. "This is the New Heroine's beautiful national ad," she said.

Her audience broke into happy applause. There was a jingling of charm bracelets, a fluttering and a flashing of bright lacquered nails. Account executives, regional sales managers, training executives, they would be returning to their territories to pass the word to local store managers and to the seventy-five hundred saleswomen—"beauty advisers"—waiting to earn their commission behind the gleaming Lauder counters in the nation's department stores.

The company launches a whole new palette of colors for eyelids, cheekbones, lips, and nails twice a year; each new palette is wrapped in imagery, a special theme. "Greek Islands," "French Impressionists," "Primitive Worlds," and "Color Transparencies" have been some color stories of past years. "We're a company tuned to conceptualizing," June Leaman told me at the sales meeting. "We never say, 'Here's a nice little lipstick.' We say, 'Here's a great big exciting story and we want to present it to you.' "

The newly heroic colors were displayed for the group to see: "Greenwood and Greylights eyeshadow . . . a concealer . . . three lipglosses, three cheek glosses, three new shades of smokestick, in kickers which will live for the life of the color story."

Sales of the scent called Estée Super Perfume (launched in 1968) were to be boosted by its being tied in to the new campaign. There were special little paisley-print pouches filled with Estée potpourri—an innovation that brought some happy "ah"s from the women, and little sighs. The door of the room was flung wide open then. "Look who's here," June Leaman said.

Estée Lauder took some steps into the room, and stopped. She stood there smiling and looking around at the women, who had risen to applaud her. A brass band and "Hail to the Chief" would scarcely seem nicer than this jingling clapping, this abundant returning of red-lipsticked smiles. Clearly, Estée Lauder understood the Ceremonial; you'd think she had watched the Monarchy at work. She lifted one arm and moved her hand back and forth, in her own version of the Royal Wave. She was apparently somewhere in her seventies, a well-corseted figure dressed in a chemise-style dress of red-and-black poppy-patterned silk, with a matching toque-style hat. She had corn-colored hair with flipped-up ends as firmly trained as an espaliered tree; a jaunty makeup; large white teeth; and brown eyes that were strikingly alive and clear.

"Listen, girls. It's easier to get to the top than to stay there," she said, in a New York voice. "You can have the finest product in the world, but if you don't go to sell it it's worth nothing." She wore big diamond ear clips and a diamond pin shaped like a swan. Her hat was draped around the crown and was covered with a red veil. Over one ear was a rosette effect, which seemed to nod for emphasis as she addressed the women—not always distinguishing them from the waiting seventy-five hundred back at home. "When you stop talking, you've lost your customer. When you turn your back, you've lost her. Touch a face. Touch a hand. Say, 'This is for you, this is what I want *you* to wear.' When you're finished, show her her face in a mirror. But don't forget, girls, hold the mirror up—up here. If you hold it down here, she looks terrible, and you've lost her."

The monologue gathered momentum as it rolled along, a stream-of-consciousness performance incorporating slogans, exhortations, memories, tales of glows natural or artificial, rose masks, a hundred and forty-four tubes of hand cream in Michigan some thirty years ago. "Beautiful, the most fantastic fragrance that ever hit the world. . . . Say, 'You know, Mrs. Lauder comes from a family of skin doctors.' . . . There was Germaine Monteil, Helena Rubinstein—all gone. I'm the only one left. . . . Try to walk in a hat, it makes you look like someone. . . . When I got started, they were selling apples on the street for a nickel, but women came to me, because I touched their faces." She turned, wearing her hat, to the door. "Remember, there's no such thing as bad business. If you don't sell, it's not the product that's wrong, it's *you,*" she said as she sailed out.

AT THE ruby-lit, winter-velvety Christmas luncheon, Estée Lauder presented me with nice, woman-to-woman quotations as if they were hors d'oeuvres. She told me all about Beautiful.

"It's like when you were a little girl, you have a rich aunt, she goes to Europe all the time, she smells beautiful, she has wonderful furs."

Each place setting had a little gift package wrapped in Christmas paper and trimmed with small brass bells. There was a mimeographed card, in the handwriting of Bob Barnes—Robert J. Barnes, president of Estée Lauder U.S.A. Candles in glass pots flickered by each plate, their flames reflected in the shiny round balls.

"These are what I call table lights," Estée Lauder said, giving a candle a proprietary push two inches to the right. "I have them in Palm Beach." Estée Lauder has luxurious houses in New York City; eastern Long Island; Palm Beach, Florida; the French Riviera; and Eaton Square, in London. Particularly before she was widowed, in 1983, she was known to throw grand parties for rich, titled, and even royal guests. Not for nothing was "Upstairs, Downstairs" one of her favorite television programs.

"I'm very good at naming," she said. "I named Age-Controlling Creme. Night Repair. Re-Nutriv. All the lipsticks. I named Youth Dew, years ago. I think up names in the middle of the night. I call up my son, Leonard, and say, 'Please have it registered immediately.' "

There was a pause. She smiled, and put her hand over mine. Lowering her voice, she asked if I was married. "Look for a sweet person," she said protectively. "Forget rich."

Then Ira Levy, senior vice-president, corporate marketing, was on his feet, making expansive gestures at a slide-projection screen. A slight, quick man with a close-trimmed beard and an adventurous yet fastidious style of dress, he was wearing, to "present" Christmas '85, a look of childlike rapture. Levy likes to term himself a frustrated architect who happens to design cosmetic packages; the gold-tone lipstick case shaped like a postmodern column was a recent inspiration. Now he had supervised the creation of all kinds of novel containers for Lauder products to give as this year's holiday gifts. It seemed that the theme had to do with art.

"Painterly brushstrokes," Levy was saying, telegraphically. "We looked at Mark Rothko. We looked at Matisse." Deftly eliding, conceptualizing, conjuring a mood, he linked themes of Japanese simplicity and neo-tsarist ornament which might, in clumsier hands, have seemed at odds. "It was Mrs. Lauder who said 'Let's make Christmas *looser*! Let's make Christmas *younger*!' " he told the sales executives. "Red is the symbol of our Christmas this year. Red is very important to Mrs. Lauder."

There was a concerted tinkling of the small brass bells as Estée Lauder rose to speak; it wasn't quite as heartwarming as applause.

"This is the first day of Christmas," she sang out, undeterred. "That's why I'm dressed like this. Today is Christmas. Today is the time to sell. Remember, it's easier to get to the top than to stay there. We have a lot of competition, but we are the original. We had our picture of the girl sleeping one way, for the advertisement for our Night Repair; another company gets some old cream and does an advertisement with a girl sleeping on the other side." She folded her hands as if in prayer, laid them first along one cheek and closed her eyes, like the model for Night Repair: Cellular Recovery Complex (a very successful Lauder product), then along the other, like the model for the competing cosmetic manufacturer. A wave of knowing laughter rocked the room. "Ha! They don't know what to do," Estée Lauder said, joining in the laughter and leaning forward to slap her manicured hands against the poppy-printed skirt.

SECRETS are the essence of the beauty business. Estée Lauder's age is as big a secret as the financial figures of her family-held corporation or the final-two-percent ingredient in the formula of Beautiful. With zest, she told the sales meeting that a published article had claimed she was eighty-five, and that she had wanted to demand a correction. Leonard Lauder, her elder son—he is fifty-three, and president and chief executive officer of the corporation—had dissuaded her. "He says, 'No, Mother, let them think you're eighty-five and you look so young and pretty. It's good for business,' " she said.

At his death in 1983, Joseph H. Lauder had been Estée Lauder's partner for over fifty years. Their son Ronald is eleven years his brother's junior; after serving for some time as head of Estée Lauder International, he left to work for the Reagan Administration, and is currently the American ambassador to Austria. "He says, 'You can't have two bosses, Mother, and Leonard wants to be the boss,' " their mother told me once, with some regret. In the late nineteen-fifties, when Leonard joined his parents in the business, there was still a mere handful of products, including some made from recipes handed down by Estée Lauder's uncle, a refugee from Hungary. "It was a modest, fine business, with a husband in the factory, six people in the office, and a wife out selling on the road," Leonard Lauder's wife, Evelyn, has said. Since that time, the business has expanded ferociously and at an ever-increasing pace. Today, the corporation, Estée Lauder Inc., consists of Estée Lauder U.S.A.; Estée Lauder International; Aramis, making cosmetic products for men; Clinique, producing an innovative "hypoallergenic" line, introduced in 1968; and the newest Lauder venture, a company called Prescriptives. Lauder companies dominate the market for high-priced cosmetics in this country's department stores and are ranked around fourth on the world market.

Profits in the cosmetic industry are dramatic; competition is cutthroat; espionage, though rarely as blatant as that employed by the late Charles Revson, of Revlon, continues rife. Lauder keeps its corporate secrets, and Estée Lauder keeps her private ones. In the past, she excelled at garnering publicity (often, as she built her business, making up the faces of women who wrote stories about her) while still maintaining a mystique. Many customers vaguely accepted her as some European aristocrat, perhaps already dead; or they confused her with the beautiful young women who represented the company image in her advertisements. But at the time of the sales meeting an unauthorized biography was known to be in the works. And Estée Lauder had been going through family albums and getting help with the writing for a book that would present her own version of her life. Along with Beautiful and the Christmas gifts, some of her secrets would be coming out.

.   .   .

THE field executives filed into a room set up like a stylized laboratory, so they could understand how Beautiful came to be. There was a distillation apparatus, with the cutest wiggles of glass condenser coils and rose oil–filled flasks. Evelyn Lauder was putting on a white coat for the session, with the rest. A brunette with a lively manner and a radiant smile, she is the vice-president of Estée Lauder Inc., and has worked for the company since 1959. She told me that her mother-in-law is a famous "nose." "She talks about seeing fragrance, tasting it," Evelyn Lauder said. She had herself developed a nose briefly—twice, when she was expecting her two sons. (The pair are in their twenties now: young Gary Lauder is a venture capitalist, while his elder brother, William, has just joined the family firm.)

"Beautiful is our eighth fragrance for women—the first since White Linen and Cinnabar, in 1978," Evelyn Lauder said. The most successful Lauder scent of all time was Youth Dew, which Estée Lauder created—first as a bath oil, on the theory that women would have no inhibitions about buying that for themselves—in 1953. "Youth Dew is the largest-selling fragrance in the world," Evelyn Lauder said. "It has sold more than Chanel No. 5. More than Arpège."

It was afternoon, but the faces of the women looked as freshly made up as they had at a peppy breakfast session that morning, when Leonard Lauder challenged them to help put a gold lipstick in every handbag in the country. They sat listening while a young woman in a peach silk dress told them about a creative process involving carnations, ambergris, civet, olibanum, jasmine, and tonka bean. They learned that twenty thousand pounds of tuberose petals make a single, ten-thousand-dollar pound of essential oil. Rebecca McGreavy, senior vice-president, corporate public relations, had eased off her gold ear clips—an unbuttoned gesture quite out of keeping—and was taking notes. Atlanta-bred, with a face to fit an oval frame on the wall of some antebellum drawing room, she wears after a long career of high-level hovering a permanent expression of iron-willed hesitancy. It comes as a surprise that she does not carry short white gloves. "French *Vogue* gave a little party for us one May Day when we were in Paris," she whispered to me, dreamily sniffing at some dried muguet, which was No. 12 on a little tray. There was a clicking of fancy fingernails on miniature mason jars as the women all around her did the same.

"Close your eyes now," said the peach-clad leader of the olfactory meditation session. "Tell me what you smell."

Her audience put nose to jars filled with vermicelli-like strings of vetiver, and sniffed.

"Peanut butter," said a voice, dutifully free-associating.

"Mushrooms," said a second.

"Xeroxing fluid," someone said when patchouli's turn came.

"I smell a wet newspaper," someone else said, when it was myrrh.

Without the genius of Estée Lauder to concoct the secret formula, nothing smelled quite right. She came through the door now, to tell them that one ounce of Beautiful contained the essence of two thousand flowers. "And that's a fact. An honest fact," she said. She told these women about the rich aunt, too, and how the perfume got its name. "I was in Palm Beach. I tried it on one of my friends, she said. 'That's beautiful, what are you going to call it?' I tried it on another lady, she said, 'Oh, Estée, that's beautiful, what are you calling it?' I said, 'You said it.' She says, 'What?' I say, 'Beautiful. That's what I'm calling it. Beautiful.'"

FRAGRANT from their baths, in clouds of Beautiful, the conferees gathered later for their Beautiful Ball.

"The field executives have been asked to wear something pastel," Rebecca McGreavy had told me as I was packing to join them. "It can be short or long."

Rustling like pale water lilies in full-skirted chiffon, silk, or spangled net, they clustered happily in little knots. Crystal facets rainbow-flashed from earlobes under cunningly fixed evening hair. Like Degas dancers, they came to peek and whisper round the doorjamb of the waiting ballroom, made pink and white since ruby lunchtime, as by fairy wand. From Kansas City, Missouri; Orlando, Florida; Greensboro, North Carolina; and Bangor, Maine, they told each other they looked beautiful. Most had risen through the ranks.

"It's great to go back and say you were with Mrs. Lauder."

"She loves the beauty advisers, she never forgets them."

"She touched all our hands."

Estée Lauder was in a floor-length dress of hand-screened pink-and-white silk, with matching scarf, and carrying opera-length white kid gloves. "Don't they look pretty?" she said, waving graciously at the Degas women. "I'm the only one in the entire world to talk to the girls, you know. No one else can do it. They write me letters, too. They're very clever."


ALVIN Chereskin, the president of the advertising agency AC&R, was sitting in the solarium of the Woodcliff Lake Hilton the following morning finishing his breakfast. He had a large, strong, bald head, and he sported a flamboyant breast-pocket handkerchief. He has worked in collaboration with June Leaman on Lauder advertising for the past twenty years. After paying tribute to his client Leonard Lauder ("People of great wealth with drive like that—it's rare. We're not talking about an Edsel here"), he told me that the cosmetic industry is one of the fastest-growing industries in the country. "And working women are going to make the industry even bigger," he said. He spoke rapidly, and sometimes stabbed the air for emphasis. "You know, I remember my mother—well, I remember her not looking too terrific sometimes. Then I remember how different she looked when she was going out for an evening. The hair, the dress, the makeup. Ta-ra! Transformed. That doesn't happen anymore."

Indeed, the women seated at the breakfast tables all around us looked as bright of lip and lid as they had the previous midnight at the ball. (Estée Lauder, who had lingered to the last with undiminished energy, was still secluded in her suite, presumably without her makeup on.)

"We've been talking about it for years, but Americans are finally discovering fragrance," Chereskin said. "They really are consuming that now. We're just such a *consuming* public in this country. Books, culture, travel, whatever—we love to spend on ourselves." Chereskin himself is a man with four homes, five cars, and a standing order for batches of books selected for him by Heywood Hill, the booksellers in London's Curzon Street.

I asked him whether wrinkles might not become socially acceptable now that all the baby-boomers were heading for middle age.

Chereskin took off like a rocket. "Let's face it, we all want to look good," he said, practically bouncing in his seat. "We don't want to get old." He reached out and gave my shoulder a little push. "Do *you* want to get fat? Don't you go to the dentist? We don't *want* to get old. Old means ugly. It means depending on other people. It means losing control. That's what frightens us. Oh, no. Staying young is going to stay with us, believe me."

.   .   .

THE stage was set. A department-store cosmetic counter stood at the far end of the hotel conference room, looking oddly stranded and out of context, like a chest of drawers in a Surrealist's desert. Banners of pink fabric hung from the ceiling above the counter and covered the back wall, like some electric dawn. The counter was flanked on one side by a person-size bouquet of mixed garden flowers and on the other by a dressmaker's dummy— a headless torso on a metal pole, draped in a pink smock like the smocks that the beauty advisers would wear during the week of the perfume's launch. Ranged on the glass top of the counter and twinkling from the lights below were bottles of Beautiful—eight "stockkeeping units," familiarly known as S.K.U.s. Four vaguely Art Moderne bottles of softened rectangular shape had lift-off gold metal caps and contained one ounce, half an ounce, or a quarter of an ounce of perfume, or 3.3 ounces of the weaker solution known as eau de parfum. Half-ounce or two-and-a-half-ounce sizes of eau de parfum appeared in bottles with taller, more ovoid silhouettes and with a new spray device, called a "spray-through" cap. There was, to complete the line, a perfume spray made of gilded metal chased with a helter-skelter texture, and a refill for it. The words "Beautiful" and "Estée Lauder" (the first with a white line underneath) stood out in bold upper case, white against the straw-colored liquid. Alongside the bottles, and looming over their pale, soft shapes like flashy dance-hall partners, stood the bold new boxes: pink, undeniably, and each with a rectangular tongue of gold-metal paper at top center. This touch had recently appeared on the green boxes of Lauder for Men, another new scent, which had been launched some weeks earlier, amid a million dollars' worth of free publicity generated by a luncheon thrown by Estée Lauder at the Helmsley Palace for some hundred of "The Most Handsome Men in New York."

The field executives sat in the room, which was heady with the scent of Beautiful and summer flowers. Images were spattering a screen once more.

"What is beautiful?" A playful, urbane voice was inquiring, through a mike. "A lake. A flower. A piece of fruit. A woman."

Alvin Chereskin paced back and forth in front of the screen, then stopped. "Our competition is almost fixated on the use of shock and gimmicks," he told the group, apparently referring to the designer Calvin Klein, who had just launched a scent called Obsession. The advertising campaign, photographed by Bruce Weber, had introduced to the pages of women's magazines hazy images of nudity and group sex. For the more prudish television networks, there had been commercials by Richard Avedon bowdlerizing the debauchery into sketches of attractive, fully clothed people involved in eccentric misbehavior. The line of evil chic begun with Saint Laurent's Opium, of 1977, had recently led to the introduction of Decadence, by the perfume division of Chesebrough-Pond's. And scheduled to appear on the market around the same time as Beautiful was Poison, by Christian Dior.

"The name Beautiful is an affirmation of the positive in an environment that dwells on the negative," Chereskin said as the room lights were dimmed and the darkness swelled with the sound of Joe Cocker singing "You Are So Beautiful." A closeup of the head of Willow Bay, half smiling and wearing a bridal veil, loomed into focus on the screen. (There was also a message reading "This is your moment to be Beautiful" and a picture of the bottle.) The watching women gasped.

"Oh, my gosh," said someone, in a Southern voice.

"This is twenty feet of tulle and lace and wonderful little pearls," June Leaman said. "Willow has finally come of age for us, with this photograph."

Willow Bay was twenty-one, and had been appearing sporadically in Lauder advertisements since she was nineteen. She was gradually edging out Karen Graham, a beauty now in her thirties, who for the past thirteen years had been the photographic model summing up the Estée Lauder image. A succession of young women have represented the Estée Lauder image over the past twenty-five years, but the eye behind the camera has remained always the same—that of the Chicago-based photographer Victor Skrebneski.

It fell to Monroe Alechman, Ira Levy's second-in-command, to tell of Beautiful's bottles and the last-minute package redesign. He was a slender man wearing purple socks and a nervous expression, and his exquisitely tailored suits (together with the flair as a dancer which he had demonstrated at the ball) turned him into a kind of Fred Astaire. He spoke animatedly about "art objects," "forms," and an "ideology reflective of Mrs. Lauder's concept." In conclusion, he asked valiantly, "Are we excited and looking pink? We are, we really are."

Estée Lauder, the impetuous colorist, was today wearing the same dress she had worn for the Most Handsome Men—it was a white silk Bill Blass, with a red feather print—and had a little red veiling cap on the espaliered hair. "He didn't tell you the whole story," she said, resting a hand on a freestanding four-foot-high version of the pink-and-gold box. "I got them all crazy yesterday. Everything was so different. 'This is how the box will be, Monroe, do you hear?'" She laughed. "It's because I'm Hungarian; I love life," she said. "I think you should start telling your customers about Beautiful right away. And when you spray them put the sample on their right hand. Your right hand is what you eat with, it's what you comb your hair with. They'll smell it more if you put it there. You know what I say is only good sense."

Then, lightheartedly, like a bride herself, she made her exit, first tossing at the happy group the Palm Beach naming, the rich aunt, and the two thousand flowers.

•   •   •

BEHIND doors all down the hallway, other seminars were taking place at the same time: on the training of the beauty adviser; on getting free publicity; on the arcana of "gift with purchase," known as G. with P.—free samples for a customer who spends a certain amount—and "purchase with purchase" (P. with P.), or special, often noncosmetic products promoted to a customer who buys cosmetics. The executives sat around skirted tables (a couple of the women took the chance to kick off their high-heeled pumps) and tossed around ideas about marketing promotions with names such as Great Assurances, Major Achievers, and Instant Rewards. Like some splendid insect queen, Estée Lauder descended on the rooms, sparked laughter and applause, and left again. Bob Barnes flung wide the doors before her, urging the groups to their feet for jingling ovations, and closed the doors behind her at the end. He was a solid, compactly built, India-rubber sort of man in a conservative navy-blue suit.

"Call your customer on a rainy day," she told one roomful. "Don't call her on a nice day, because she won't be home."

"I was supposed to be in Europe," she told a different group. "But I stayed to be with you. I'm leaving next week to be with Prince Charles and Lady Di. We're sponsoring him in a polo match. I hope he appreciates it. I hope he wins."

At Estée Lauder, everything ties in. Beautiful, and Christmas, and the new Skin Perfecting Creme: Firming Nourisher, and the story of the founder's life—all were moving onto the market in an interdependent convoy, like a string of barges.

"Be sure to tell your customer it has Firmex and that it works together with Night Repair," she told her listeners.

"I wasn't a New York person, I came from a small town. But I fought! . . . 'Face-lifting without a knife,' it was called, in German, a special facial pack . . . 'The House of Ash Blondes,' that's where I got my start. It was cash before delivery in those days. Now it's an empire!"

One of these rooms had a stranded sales counter, too. Seeing Estée Lauder bustle into position around the end of it and stand behind it moving some jars and bottles a few inches this way or that was like seeing a brain surgeon scrub up. And her dialogue with an imaginary customer seemed to reflect youthful dreams of acting on the stage. "You say, 'I have a glow of a base that's so perfect you're going to love it. I have something that's going to make you look young and fresh.' She says, 'What's that?' As soon as you say 'young and fresh,' you've got her. Keep talking. Don't look down. Look right into her face. And when you give her a sample don't just hand it to her or throw it into her shopping bag. Give it to her like it's precious. Say, 'This is for you. This is what I want you to try.' "

Barnes came bouncing into the hallway at her heels, rubbing his hands.

"That's the kind of stuff they love!" he said, his eyes alight. "That's what I want. Sell! Sell! Sell!"

THE spotlight of attention was the most flattering of cosmetics: as Estée Lauder stepped among the eager, waiting faces, the years fell away. In the no man's land of the hallway, she seemed to age. She sat down on a banquette—carefully, so as not to crease the feather-printed skirt—and called for a cup of coffee. She patted the place beside her, and I sat down as well.

"My father came from a lovely family," she said. "My mother always said to me, 'Your hands! Take care of your hands.' In Europe, when a man kisses your hand he knows all your background from it. My mother was always brushing her hair. Even as a young girl, I only wanted beauty. All for beauty. I don't know where I got that from." She looked dreamy, weary, misty-eyed.

"Fetch me one of those Blockbusters!" she said, rallying and summoning a nearby aide. It was a P. with P. for the new season—a white plastic box about the size of a briefcase, with multiple molded compartments, like an airline dinner tray. Estée Lauder set it on her lap, prized open the lid, and looked down. There were virginal sample quantities of cosmetics—a palette of blue, brown, lilac, green, rose pink, red. "Look at that. How lovely that is," Estée Lauder said. "We lose a lot of money on it. It sells for nineteen ninety-five. At retail, it's a hundred-and-twenty-five-dollar value." She swept her hand over the colors, pointing out a glow.

"All Mrs. Lauder's promotions have a glow," the aide said.

"I always say glow comes from health, from underneath the skin," Estée Lauder said.

We sat side by side, looking down at the white plastic tray. "Isn't that beautiful?" she said.

Then she dispatched the aide for a bottle of Night Repair. "Restores damaged cells. Only a few drops, that's all you need," she said. "Sells for forty or fifty dollars. Saks can't keep it in stock." She pressed the little brown bottle into my hand and closed my fingers over it. "Put it in your pocketbook," she said.

"THE creation of anything at Estée Lauder is more of a team effort than anyone can understand," Leonard Lauder said to me. "No one woman can say, 'I see pink!' or whatever. That's not the way things work anymore."

There had been hints at the sales meeting that the new scent had not been christened Beautiful without a lot of anguish among the management team, just as Beautiful had not turned pink with ease. We were sitting in Lauder's office at corporate headquarters, on the thirty-seventh floor of the General Motors building, on Fifth Avenue. Enough weeks had passed for the ruffled feathers to have settled down.

"We have had the actual fragrance for some time," he said. "With this one, we had some difficulty with the name, the presentation, the positioning in the market, the packaging." He had his mother's warm brown eyes and her smile, which in his case turned up at the corners, for a puckish touch. A habit of shooting his eyebrows upward had left a tracery of wrinkles on his broad brow. For all his charm, he seemed a determined man.

"It was Carol Phillips, the president of Clinique, who first thought of the name," he said. "Mrs. Lauder reacted positively to Beautiful right away, and I have learned to rely on her original instincts. We checked it out in the world market. Evelyn Lauder was always in favor of Beautiful. I liked Beautiful because, one, it was audacious, and, two, it had a built-in position. Position? That means the creation of a concept that will properly present a product to the consumer. A classic position would be the Volkswagen bug: a small car, maintenance-free." He spoke fast, sometimes punctuating with a professorial "Now." "Obsession has a built-in position: it's sexy. Our own White Linen has a built-in position: it's crisp. We had code-named the new fragrance Project Elle, but we didn't really want to use Elle, because it was the name of a magazine and because we felt that the market had gone beyond that. We also considered E.L., but we felt that that was too conservative. We had the two-thousand-flowers idea, something like Mille Fleurs, and we had Eté, the French word for summer, but that was too close to White Linen and it looked like a misspelling of Estée."

Leonard Lauder's private life—whether jogging, opera going, reading, art collecting, or skiing in Aspen, where he has a house—seems somehow purposeful and hungry, like his style at work. Even the oblivion of sleep is harnessed, like the waters at a hydroelectric dam. "The fragrance was approved sometime in January," he said. "Mrs. Lauder felt good about it. Evelyn Lauder felt good about it. They called me up—woke me up, as a matter of fact. I was in Europe, and they got the time wrong. After that, the name was this for a while, then it was that. In March, I was in Aspen, Mrs. Lauder was in Palm Beach, everyone else was in New York. I said, 'Look. I'll be in New York on Wednesday. By Friday, I'll make the decision.' Mrs. Lauder said, 'Fine, I'm tired of all this.' She's a good trouper. We're a good team—if you lose, you're still going to go ahead and get behind the product. On Friday at five, I went over to a space we have at 660 Madison with Ira Levy, June Leaman, Evelyn Lauder, Bob Barnes. I still liked the audacity of Beautiful, and I decided on that. Now, we also decided on the blue-and-white packaging design that day. But somehow on the way to the package it lost a lot of its original energy and strength. And after about the fiftieth time I looked at the package I was feeling really uncomfortable with it. Mrs. Lauder said it seemed O.K. to her, but I was still uncomfortable. Then, on the Saturday before the sales meeting, I took a nap. While sleeping, I dreamed of a new package theme: the theme of Lauder for Men, but done throughout our fragrance line. Yes, I just had a dream! Like Jacob in the Bible. I have learned to listen to my dreams. It doesn't happen very often, but whenever it does the result has been a fabulous commercial success. Once, I dreamed that our competitor had a new product that had never been done before. I woke up all upset. Then I realized it was only a dream, and they had no such product. So we made it ourselves, and it was a great success. I called Mrs. Lauder to tell her about my dream for Beautiful. I said, 'I want to do a blue-and-white package but with a pink liner and a gold tongue, like Lauder for Men.' And she said, 'Fine, but I want to make it pink on the outside, too.' "

· · ·

"WHEN she said 'pink,' it was like being hit in the stomach," Ira Levy told me, in his office, at around the same time. "Mrs. Lauder *hated* pink for years. But Mrs. Lauder is amazing. She has the ability to galvanize people. She's kept *me* galvanized for twenty years. She sees everything, you know. When she's in Europe, even if she's only in her car being driven down the King's Road, you may be sure she has her nose pressed to the glass. The other day, she was telling me about being at the races at Longchamp and watching some baronne—de Rothschild, I think it was —get out a big white compact. Round like a saucer, Mrs. Lauder said it was, like Rita Hayworth's compact. I knew everything about that compact from the way she told me—about how the woman took out the puff and just went like this." He did an imitation of Mrs. Lauder's imitation of the woman expansively applying her powder puff.

Packages for Estée Lauder skin treatments and makeup have tradi- tionally been a discreet robin's-egg blue (referred to reverentially as Estée Lauder blue) ornamented only by the founder's forceful signature, in gold. But the packages for Estée Lauder Sun, a 1985 line of products to promote or prevent suntanned skin, had dramatically broken through the tranquil aquamarine line. "Mrs. Lauder said, 'I want bright yellow!' " Levy said, with an imperious gesture of his whole arm. " 'No. Brighter. Like the *sun*!' " The line had been a commercial success, giving the company courage. "If this were two years ago, and you'd shown me that pink, I would have said, 'It's not right for Lauder, it'll upset the balance of nature on our counters.' But design is about change. Just think: if this were 1972 and we were to show a bridal ad, Gloria Steinem would be leading a march to the barricades. But this is what is around us now. We are bourgeois, but with zappy accents: the new bourgeoisie, in their co-op lofts, with very proper, conservative table linen, serving—oh, scallops on a bed of pumpkin purée with shiitake mushrooms, or something."

Levy told me he had been among the majority of the inner circle of management who had resisted the name Beautiful. "I found it hard to focus on it, I was embarrassed by it," he said. "For a woman to wear a fragrance called Beautiful . . . I kept saying, 'But what if she's *not* beautiful?' I liked Eté for a name. It related to Estée, and to summer as a state of mind."

Time heals all, and he was able to give an amicable shrug. "That's the creative process here," he said. "We're allowed to develop our own positions and then fight it out. Of course, this is a political place. It's like a court. But I happen to like life at court." He had a twinkle in his eye. I could easily picture him in doublet and hose.

He began flipping through the pages of a book of photographs of life and art in Japan, soaking up the images with a look at once ecstatic and businesslike. There was a page with a blue, blue sea and fishing nets in lines like jewels, and a second page with a blue-and-white wave design.

"That's what was going down the line," Monroe Alechman said, pausing as he passed through the room to glance over Levy's shoulder. "The rest is history."

"I have tried very hard to get the focus on the simple kind of beautiful, the more Japanese kind of beautiful," Levy said. "The Japanese have this word *'shibui'*—a concept of taste, harmony. The beauty of thoughts and words, like haiku. Minimal things, like the Imperial Gardens."

The broken pediment at the top of the A.T. & T. Building was outside the window beyond his head. He had recently finished working on his dream house in Connecticut, based on his own neo-Palladian ideas. "I sense that I am changing," he said. "I am turning my eyes in the direction of the spiritual now. Perhaps it is because I am in touch with nature. Just this morning, when I woke up and looked out on the patio I saw three deer."

•    •    •

Rebecca McGreavy and her public-relations staff were kept busy in the summer months before the launch.

"The most fun thing of a launch is getting the fragrance into the hands of people who'll enjoy it," she told me, in her magnolia-blossom voice, describing one aspect of a formidable machinery. Estée Lauder was still in Europe; I looked into her empty office, with its Louis XVI furniture and its opulent silk curtains and its generous Central Park view. There was a portrait of a happy-looking Estée Lauder dancing with her husband, taken by Norman Parkinson. He had also photographed her for the story on Beautiful to appear in the October *Town & Country*. Mrs. Lauder had been in Paris at the time of the new portrait, attending a Beautiful orientation meeting of Estée Lauder International's general managers. There had been the pink-and-white dress with the scarf, and what Rebecca McGreavy called "a floral tribute even more lovely" than the New Jersey version, and Parks running around the Plaza Athénée in his funny little embroidered hat. For the sitting, he had linked up scarf and flowers most imaginatively. "He got a little carried away with the scarf," Rebecca McGreavy said.

On an end table by a plump silk-covered sofa was a framed snapshot of Estée Lauder arm in arm with George Bush. There were also photographs of her beaming away with the President.

Phyllis Melhado, the public-relations officer for Estée Lauder U.S.A., came to join us. She has a mass of dark wavy hair, which she wears sometimes (as on this occasion) pulled back and sometimes on her shoulders, loose and free; her hobby is horseback riding. The two women looked at each other, then back at me.

"Shall we begin in the little room, do you think, Phyllis?" Rebecca McGreavy said.

A windowless room some twelve feet square had been specially consecrated to instructing the fashion press about the new scent. Pink walls cast a glow on us and on the yellow-filled bottles that stood on a glass tabletop next to another lavish arrangement of flowers. A white peony had let fall some petals onto the glass, and a pinch of egg yolk–colored pollen. The scent was overpowering.

The birth of Beautiful would be marked by an advertisement financed jointly by Estée Lauder Inc. and the Neiman-Marcus stores, which would run in newspapers in Texas on Sunday, September 15. Department stores all over the country would be running their jointly financed newspaper advertisements between September 22 and October 13. The company's bride would simultaneously begin fluttering into the magazines of the nation and the world, like confetti. Along with what Rebecca McGreavy called the "salvo of advertising," the heavy artillery was to be mobilized: Estée Lauder herself would sally forth to the cities of Washington and Dallas sometime after Labor Day.

"Don't call them 'personal appearances,' " Rebecca McGreavy said. "Mrs. Lauder will merely *be* in those cities at the time of the launch."

Evelyn Lauder, for her part, would go to Boston and Chicago, giving interviews and appearing at Jordan Marsh and Marshall Field's. And, between them, Rebecca McGreavy and Phyllis Melhado were personally instructing several hundred women—the country's writers on topics of fashion and beauty—beginning with those from glossy magazines with months-long lead times and moving on through the weeklies to the daily papers.

"We don't really have to *teach* them," Phyllis Melhado said.

"It's an interplay," Rebecca McGreavy said. "It's fun to present Beautiful, because of their enthusiasm. Beautiful as a fragrance has been *loved.*"

The pair seemed to vibrate with excitement in the little room; they tripped over each other's sentences.

"When they walk in here, they always go, 'Ooh, isn't this beautiful.' "

"We let them stand there and look. Then we say, 'Mrs. Lauder says it takes two thousand fresh flowers to make a single ounce of Beautiful.' "

"We spray it on them. We spray it on us. We talk about the bottles, and the packaging."

"All the while oohing and ahing about the way our wrists smell."

"We stroke the bottle and say we think of it as a touchstone."

The two had had to make some changes in their wardrobes.

"Phyllis and I love to wear red. But you can't really wear red next to pink," Rebecca McGreavy said.

"Rebecca found a pink dress," Phyllis Melhado said. "I'm sticking with white for now."

Down the hallway, in what the two women referred to as the big room—a much larger, conference-size room, set up to present Beautiful to the representatives of retail stores—we met up with Bob Barnes. He sat down at another glass-topped table and folded his arms; he wore a heavy gold signet ring with a yellow stone.

"Everyone in America is going back to being married," he said. "They are respecting the American flag more." He unfolded his arms and brought his hands together with a manly clapping sound. "We really think we have some tremendous tie-ins here," he said. "If a lady ever looks good, it's going to be on her wedding day."

The table was set with a silver coffeepot, pretty pastries, and books artfully opened at Redouté roses and Harry Winston gems.

"This is positively the biggest, strongest promotional effort we have ever made," he said. "Lots of electronic media. Lots of direct mail. Inserts in all the magazines and in catalogues. Presidential letters." These last were letters sent out by store presidents to charge-account customers asking them to try the scent. Estée Lauder provided a draft, which might be "signed" by the presidents or by Estée Lauder herself. "One store wants four hundred thousand," Barnes said. "They are so enthusiastic they want to tell the world."

There was a store counter along one wall, in full Beautiful regalia. Not just the bottles, boxes, and smock by now but all the "collaterals," or promotional accessories—pink-and-gold paper shopping bags in four-inch and fourteen-inch sizes; plastic countertop display stands shaped like tongues of hot-pink flame, to hold test-spray bottles; the gold-cased Re-Nutriv lipstick, Polished Performance nail lacquer, and Tender Blusher, of the special Beautiful Pink cosmetics collection; and a huge glass urn, shaped and spigoted like a samovar, for the procedure known as "dramming."

"When a customer comes into the store, she is handed a small vial and what we call a referral card," Rebecca McGreavy explained. "She takes the vial to the counter, where it will be filled with a sample of eau de parfum from the urn."

"We were the originators of dramming," Barnes said. He had folded his arms again and was looking over at the pink-and-gold panorama with some satisfaction. "It creates interest around the counter."

Willow Bay was half smiling at us from her photograph on a silvery store easel. The bride would appear in both print and television advertisements. And the song "You Are So Beautiful," rearranged and sung in what Barnes called a "more refined way" than Joe Cocker's, would be heard on radio and on television. This unity was very much of a plus, Barnes said—something different from the competition.

I asked how Obsession had affected Beautiful.

"Beautiful was in the works before they even came out with Obsession," Barnes said testily. "We've never been sensational or faddy." He had been holding the earpieces of his reading glasses together in one hand; now he opened them wide and chewed briefly on one end. "I guess you could say we are returning to things that are nice," he said, with care. "Emphasizing the positive instead of the negative."

"Mrs. Lauder believes that people are recommitting themselves to lovely traditional things," Rebecca McGreavy said, and smiled.

.  .  .

"TA-RA! Ta-ra!"

Alvin Chereskin, his head covered by a fancy silk handkerchief knotted at the four corners, stepped out from the portico of the mansion with the bride on his arm. The rest of his outfit made one think of some Hollywood director of the Josef von Sternberg era. For the television commercial, Estée Lauder Inc. had rented the mansion at a daily rate from the owner, a grandson of the industrialist and philanthropist Henry Phipps. The grand curving staircase had been used in the past for a Christmas Blockbuster commercial; the balustrade of the Italianate garden for White Linen; and the reflecting pool (with rented swans) for an advertisement for Estée Super Perfume. The rumble of the Long Island Expressway could be faintly heard from somewhere off beyond the ha-ha and the arboretum.

Willow Bay, in a fifteen-thousand-dollar bridal gown and with what was by now far more than twenty yards of tulle secured to her head with a tiara of fresh rosebuds, was emerging from a lengthy seclusion with the makeup man. Some fifty people were milling on the sloping lawns: camera and lighting people; teamsters, grips, and gofers; June Leaman (back from a trip to Provence, and wearing a T-shirt that said "Fondation Maeght"); Chereskin's copywriter and his executive art director (wearing a pink Lacoste, in honor of "the product"); a real French director, wearing Indian-style pajamas and a long ponytail; a five-year-old girl named Nicole Ganz, dressed in lace and rosebuds, as a flower girl; and Nicole Ganz's mother, in jeans. Every single one of these people, in these dog days of summer, was more or less tinged by a tan. Except Willow Bay. Her skin was milk-white, fine, translucent, like something from another world. A pale hint of lavender vein swam branchingly under the bisque, at her temple.

"You'll find most cosmetic models don't tan," David Leonard, the makeup artist, told me. "We have too much trouble matching the face and the hands if they do. And we're always working a season ahead." He had prepared the young woman by rubbing foundation on her pale neck and her chest, which was so thin you could see the soft ridges of the upper ribs. He had powdered the long, slender arms, with their down of fine blond hair. He had painstakingly painted and overpainted the canvas of her face, concealing from the world at large a tiny scar, as from a tomboy childhood, next to the outlined bow of a Beautiful Pink–lipsticked mouth.

"She looks very matte," June Leaman said. And she was fretting about a line of black pencil that Leonard had drawn along the roots of Willow Bay's lower lashes. "Her eyes are narrow. She can look squinty, if we're not careful. Especially when she's backlit."

"Action!"

Willow Bay came running out from under a tree in an ectoplasmic drift of tulle. Her course took her closely past the film camera and a cluster of ten-foot silk panels and tinfoil screens, for directing and diffusing the light of the hot summer sun.

"When she hits those silks, there will be a moment when she's beautiful," Chereskin said. He went back to shouting directions through a megaphone, grudgingly deferring to the French director and bellowing for scissors in order to add or subtract lengths of tulle.

"See that lace? The sunlight coming through? I want it. It's rich."

"Action!"

"Better!" Chereskin shouted encouragingly. "Better! Better! Nice."

A fluffy white cloud came puffing into the blue sky above the Doric columns of the white gazebo that stood at the top of the sloping lawn; he fell in love with the effect. A perfect Gainsborough, or perhaps a Constable, he said. After all, he had trained as a painter, and hadn't set out to be an advertising man. The bride ran over the lawn again. ("Like a white heifer," Willow Bay said later, with a grin. She is an intelligent young woman, with a college degree.)

"I've had two weddings, and neither of them was remotely like this," June Leaman said, looking on from a lawn chair. The pale arms were pumping, the knees pushing up under the snowy skirts. It would look more romantic when the film was run in slow motion.

"Willow is really of the eighties," Chereskin said, dropping into a canvas chair and mopping at his face. "She's a big girl, with today's androgynous look. She's not even perfect featured. But who's perfectly beautiful these days anyway? Elizabeth Taylor was probably the last of the great beauties. Even the legendary Hollywood beauties were very careful about how they were filmed or photographed. Probably had it all written into their contracts. Did you know that Claudette Colbert insisted on being shot from one side, her best side? If you can find a shot of the wrong side of Claudette Colbert's face, I'll give you a hundred dollars."

The French director had to consult Chereskin about the storyboard. "Zee little girl, she is also running?"

Now, like a foal at the flank of its mare, the child came trotting in white satin slippers next to the speeding bride. Rosebuds ringed a fluff of spun-gold hair; multicolored ribbons from her posy streamed behind her as she ran.

"She likes it when she can look pretty," the child's mother said, watching. "I called yesterday to make sure she was really going to be on camera this time. Last time, they had another little girl, who was Nicole's double, and they went with her. Nicole kept asking when it was going to be *her* turn. She's old enough to understand rejection, and I can't put her through that again."

Between takes, the child was burying her button-shaped, kitten-pink nose in the bouquet, then looking out of the corner of her eye to see if any grownups were watching her.

"She goes to two or three auditions a week," her mother said. "I tell her all the kids can't get the job, and she understands that. She's done five or six commercials. Peanut Clusters. Shuffletown toys. She was an extra on Hi-C."

Nicole came skipping over to her mother and reached for the biggest of the strawberries on a nearby plate.

"Was that fun, the running?" the woman asked, fluffing her daughter's lace sleeves and setting the rosebuds straight on her head. "I saw you follow your direction very well." Firmly, she separated her daughter from the strawberry, which was dripping juice.

"Did you see when I looked up at the bride?" the little girl asked.


"I DON'T think decadence is wrong," Alvin Chereskin was saying. "I think it's kind of kicky and cute."

We were now indoors, where the remaining split-second scenes were to be shot, in a tall, white-curtained second-floor room with a Biedermeier mirror standing on a parquet floor. Powerful movie lighting, more reliable and more flattering than mere sun, was directed in through the windows from platforms planted on hydraulic stilts on the gravelled garden path. Chereskin leaned his elbow on a mantel in a pause while the lighting people trimmed their arcs.

"Obsession was brave, different, daring," he said. "It took a stance. But it was Obsession by Calvin Klein. You couldn't have Obsession by Estée Lauder."

As a creative man, Chereskin had to push the limits, just the same. He had wanted to try some scenes with an unclothed bride, gauzily veiled, contemplating her own beauty in the mirror. "Sex! What is that but *life*, after all?" Chereskin asked. "We're all of us selling sex, because we're all selling life. Of course, Calvin is going beyond sex. He's trying to legitimize things normally hidden. But all of us have some little black hole deep in the psyche. You can't control your fantasies, your dreams. We're all voyeurs, to some extent."

Indeed, a Peeping Tom was standing outside the upstairs window now, manning his film lamp and peeking from behind big, wilting branches of camouflaging shrubbery. But the idea of gauzy nakedness, even with a flesh-colored bodystocking, had been vetoed in advance by the taste committees at the television networks.

June Leaman was resolutely opposed as well. "Alvin's like a dog with a bone sometimes," she said. "I have to say, 'Alvin, let *go*.'"

Willow Bay, wearing her bridal veil over a rather graceless beige silk undershirt and French pants—a compromise, but visible clothing, at least —waited in an adjacent cool green room. She sat crouched on a little footstool, her arms locked around her skinny knees, and looking wraith-like under a pyramid of tulle that ended in a cascade of spume all around her on the green rug. David Leonard sat knee to knee with her, whisper-ing like her confessor and from time to time reaching with his tail comb under the tabernacle of the veil to tweak at some lock of hair.

The heat of the lamps had cracked the Biedermeier mirror. Desper-ate telephoning went on. The only substitute had already been requisi-tioned for the set of "All My Children." Lieutenants were sent off in search of a local glazier. Chereskin, saying he was very superstitious and Russian peasant about these things, slumped in a chair, threw his hand-kerchief over his face, and moaned.

The mirror was repaired. Willow Bay stepped up to it on cue, widening her eyes and crowning herself with the rosebud tiara and the veil. The camera rolled and stopped, rolled and stopped again. June Leaman stood in the doorway out of camera range and glowered. "If I were a woman turning on the TV, I'd wonder what the hell that girl was doing, standing there in her underwear," she muttered. She had earlier assured me that Chereskin's flight of fancy would not make it to the final cut. "I don't want to get any angry letters. And we feel that the pendulum is swinging back to traditional values. Group sex, ménages à trois—with the return to religion, all that will vanish. You don't find the born-again Christians going for that sort of thing."


THE manufacturing plant, warehouse, and distribution center of Estée Lauder Inc. in Melville, Long Island, are within a stone's throw of the Long Island Expressway, too—close enough that when Estée Lauder is being driven to her house on the Island she can catch a satisfactory glimpse of her name lit up high on the factory's wall. "I think, Is this all *mine*?" she told me once. And years ago, she said, there was just a little factory in New Hyde Park, whose handful of workers she would visit each day at four o'clock, bearing cakes and cookies.

At the Melville plant, by the third week of August, Beautiful was out of the starting gate and running neck and neck with the bride. Manufacture was well in hand, and distribution a matter of some urgency.

"Everyone is against the wall with something new," Jack Doran told me when I went out to visit the plant. Doran, a vice-president in charge of day-to-day operations, was a feet-on-the-ground sort of fellow with a dense thatch of ginger hair and a background in Pennsylvania and the steel business. He had been responsible for ushering Beautiful—mixed, bottled, capped, packaged, and attended by its collaterals—down the plant's production line in a schedule that was simultaneously digesting the seasonal bulge of Christmas goods. "There's a new mold for the glass shapes, and there's the color for the metallized packaging," he said. "The testers, the banners, the shopping bags—a lot of handwork, and these things are not cheap. Then, it's always impossible to predict what will catch the consumer's eye, and orders may be bigger than our forecast. We have to be sure the converters who make the bottles and the caps are ready, and the people who do the lettering. Some of the parts come from France."

Doran handed me a white disposable cap before we walked out on the factory floor, and he donned one himself; it looked as though some maverick pancake had landed on his thatch. He opened a door onto a room where lipsticks were being born. Roller mills like giant mangles ("Same as they use in the paint industry," Doran said) were slowly turning and turning—grinding powdered pigments and blending them with castor oil. The gluey mixture—red-red, orange-red, blue-red, pink, and coral—spread across the rollers, dripped slowly, slurp-slopping, into waiting pans, then came around to be rolled all over again. Along the sides of the room stood shiny round-bottomed stainless-steel caldrons, some waist high and some so tall they had metal access stairs alongside. Each caldron was labelled with a hand-scrawled sign saying "Ginger Flower," "Plum Brandy," or "Rose Mist." Men in red-smudged white shirts and pants and with pancake hats like our own moved with a scuffing of work shoes on tiled floor to mount the stairs and peer into the hot lipstick mixture, or set it swirling with big mechanical paddles. The air was blanketed with acrid, waxy-smelling steam. Here and there stood drums, barrels, and outsize ice-cream cartons—part of a constant traffic of bulk-packed raw materials and finished products travelling between the factory and the automated warehouse, some hundred yards away.

"This is your creams-and-lotions lab—your big stuff," Doran said, sidestepping what looked like a huge black oil drum but was marked "Swiss Treatment Shampoo," and entering a cavernous space filled with even larger kettles, larger drums, and swimming pool–size tanks. Here was a purposeful temple, a humming engine room of beauty, served by fat coiled pipes, broad expanses of metal platform, hoists, meters, gauges, paddles, and computerized consoles with flashing lights. Seven hundred and fifty gallons of Skin Perfecting Creme was steaming away on one side, like a huge pot of hot, pale custard. On the other, a matching pot of Greaseless Body Lotion had progressed to the stage of cooling down; condensation sparkled from the kettle's silvery rounded bottom, like big cold tears. A white-clad man was beginning a fresh operation in a third kettle, as yet empty: taking telephone-book-size slabs of white beeswax, cracking them in half against the rim, and tossing them in with an echoing boom.

Doran and I moved on to another large chamber, this one unmanned, and crowded, like some moonlit African village, with tall, silvery conical-roofed storage tanks. "There are from one thousand to three thousand gallons in each of these tanks," Doran said. "These are for the alcohol-based products—your astringents, colognes, perfumes." Somewhere, there was a tank of Beautiful. Deionized water and alcohol—far and away the largest ingredients of all such liquid beauty products—were pumped in from special tanks placed safely outside the building. This room was built to be explosion-proof: it had blowout roof hatches and a nonfriction floor. The air in here was pleasantly but indefinably sweet.

Free samples of Beautiful were to be distributed to the factory workers that evening as they left for home, Doran said.

I asked if he expected them to be excited, and he gave something like a shrug.

"You've always got some new product coming out," he said. "Fall colors, summer, sun, Christmas. They get a free gift every two months, plus they get to buy things in a boutique at discount."

A floor below the manufacturing operations, a run of Beautiful came rumbling and clicketing down the rollers of an assembly line. Some two dozen workers, almost all of them women, stood shoulder to shoulder or sat on high stools, chattering and joking as they worked. They wore cheap blouses and jeans by Calvin Klein's competitors; their names were written under the larger name of Estée Lauder on I.D. cards (with less than

Skrebneski-level photographs) pinned to the bosoms of Lauder-blue smocks. A young beauty with large dark eyes and an angelic heart-shaped face under her white cap sat at the head of the conveyor deftly unpacking empty bottles from cardboard nests and setting them upright to begin their journey down the line. The bottles first met a machine that breathed a cleansing puff of air into each with a repeated *pfff-shush, pfff-shush* sound. Then they snaked into a figure eight under an upturned carboy filled with bubbling yellow eau de parfum. A machine that bristled tubes and pistons hissed and spurted over the bottles, mechanically filling them and extracting air.

"Most alcohol products use the vacuum-fill method," Doran said. "Your heavy viscous you pump."

Hands in yellow-tinged white cotton gloves fluttered over the full bottles, setting on the gold-metal caps and then, with a half-twist and a polish, dispatching them down the line once more.

"Those caps are like jewels," Doran said, looking on.

Dozens more fluttering fingers unfolded pink-and-gold packages, gave the bottles a final rub, then nestled them in pink tissue and stashed them away. There was an unfamiliar bottom note of cardboard in humid weather, but no mistaking the smell of Beautiful by now.

"NOBODY works in here, so there's no need for lights," Doran said. We were in the automated storage and retrieval warehouse, standing with our hands on the guardrail of an observation balcony and peering into the gloom. The space yawned over our heads and in front of us like the interior of a cathedral by night. Aisles of tall metal shelving stretched away like river cliffs; shapes of drums, crates, and boxes loomed from their places near us, then vanished into the darkness farther off. Giant robotic cranes waited like attentive dogs for computerized signals to ferry or retrieve. Suddenly, a metal monster would go skidding away down the darkened aisles on some mission, humming and hissing and flashing colored lights. There were eighteen thousand component units in here, Doran said as we stood watching the robots come and go. I thought of the beeswax and the lanolin; the mineral, avocado, and castor oils; the pigments, preservatives, and powders; the Orange No. 5 and the Blue No. 1; the bottles, caps, jars, and tubes; the umbrellas, tote bags, and coat hangers given as P. with P.s; the little bottles of foundation christened Fresh Air, Perfectly Natural, and Country Mist guarding their secrets inside the robin's-egg boxes with the big gold signatures; the Tender Blushers, and the Luscious Creme Mascaras, with their little spiral brushes like those for some dollhouse chimney flue; the virgin bullet shapes of lipsticks, sheathed and waiting in their gilded postmodern tubes.

"Beautiful?" Doran said when I asked him where he thought it might be. "It could be in five or six different aisles. Stacking is random in here. If you put all of one product in one aisle and then something happened to lock you out of that aisle, you'd be out of business. The computer knows how to find the product, and that's what counts. Beautiful is just another number."

THE editing room in midtown Manhattan was also dark, but it was very small and it was crowded with real, live people: Alvin Chereskin, his art director and his copywriter for the Beautiful commercial; the producer; and Jeff Cahn, the film editor—a bearded, bearlike man in a Hawaiian shirt patterned with palm trees. Six thousand feet of film was shrinking down to forty-five, for the thirty-second spot. Everyone sat staring at the small screen, where white-draped brides and frisky flower girls were unrolling like a line of postage stamps or recklessly flinging themselves into reverse. The child looked more innocent on camera than in life; with Willow Bay, the opposite was true.

"Now, that, that's glorious. As gorgeous as it gets in life," said one of the voices in the dark when a closeup of the bride came around.

"But you can see the scar," Jeff Cahn said.

"The scar! Oh, my God, he noticed the scar!" the art director said, with a wail.

Chereskin sat on a stool behind Cahn's broad back and poked at the palm trees with a finger from time to time.

"Sky! I want to see more sky!" he said. There was a cranking sound of rewinding film. Sky showed blue, and a miniature white gazebo, like something off a wedding cake.

"But where's my cloud?" Chereskin said. There was no cloud in sight. "Oh, what a disappointment. You're killing me."

He punched Cahn on the shoulder, rocked miserably on his stool. The child in closeup lifted a sun-washed face, the kitten nose, the spun-gold hair beneath the rosebud wreath, and Willow Bay looked down. There was a gasp in the dark.

"Almost a Botticelli," Chereskin said.

Somewhere along the line, the underwear scene had been quietly dropped. Instead, the model's head was three-quarter face in closeup, with a widening eye and the curve of a blooming cheek. It seemed that Chereskin liked her with her nose tilted up, while Skrebneski liked her with her chin down; the two men were forever struggling over that.

"To me, this is a very nice shot. Almost a nun," Alvin Chereskin said, placing the pads of five splayed fingers directly on the screen, right over the young woman's face.

"The eye," he said over the background of the cranking sound. "I must see the eye. Nice. Nice. Gorgeous. Better. The smile, the flowers, the crown—Leonard will love it. Next! No, I just want the eyes. I don't need the mouth. I don't need the whole face. Picture this right after a spaghetti commercial. Spaghetti, spaghetti, spaghetti, then all of a sudden —bam! ta-ra! ta-ra!—an eye. The eye will work."

"We need four and a half seconds for the store tag," someone said, referring to the punch line of the spot, telling consumers in softened mood where to go to buy the product. "We need to lose two seconds."

"We've got to take the eyes out," Chereskin said, decisively. "Would you believe it, those damn eyes go in and out. This is giving me heartburn."


"You are so beautiful to me-ee-ee. Can't you see, You're everything I hoped for, Everything I need. You are so beautiful to me."

Marc Cohn, a baritone dressed in the style of "Miami Vice," stood in the sound booth at the recording studio, behind a dangling microphone. His voice swelled, his eyes screwed closed, his hands clung to the headphones around his ears.

"I can do that bit in falsetto, but it's not going to sound tender," he said, breaking off and speaking to the people at the soundboard beyond the glass. The music was being put in in layers: I had passed three string players with their instrument cases going out as I came in; I could hear a saxophone's preparatory tootles down the hall.

"Beautiful commercial," Cohn murmured, lingering after he was done to watch a run-through of the video together with the sound.

The Botticelli closeup of the bride and the child had also vanished; when Leonard Lauder and June Leaman saw the edited tape they had been unanimous in rejecting the shot, on the ground that the child's beauty competed with that of Willow Bay. "A little blond kid will kill anybody," June Leaman said later. "It could have been Garbo. The kid couldn't stay."

.   .   .

WHEN Estée Lauder arrived at the Dallas–Fort Worth airport shortly after Labor Day, she walked away from the group that had come to greet her and from the entourage that had travelled with her, and headed for the baggage carousel. She stood like a terrier at a rabbit hole watching for her luggage to come thundering through the rubber-flapped chute. In spite of her scattered mansions, Estée Lauder does not appear to enjoy travelling around by air. She is suspicious of airlines' promises to depart or arrive on time, and seems cautious about entrusting them with her personal property, packed with the aid of a personal maid into many unmatched and homely-looking suitcases.

Estée Lauder's "merely being" in Dallas at the time of the launch of Beautiful had all the trappings of a three-day Royal Progress. On the flight from New York, there had been her maid and her security man, and Rebecca McGreavy, doing her hovering at heightened intensity, like a lady-in-waiting to the Queen. At the airport, a string of limousines was at the ready, as were Toni Hopkins, a vice-president and divisional merchandise manager of Neiman-Marcus, and Robert Tetley, a vice-president of Estée Lauder U.S.A. and its field sales manager for all of Texas, Louisiana, Oklahoma, Mississippi, and Arkansas, as well as parts of Alabama, Kansas, and Tennessee. Tetley was a tall man with wire-rimmed spectacles and a high-pitched nervous giggle, which sat oddly with his gangling, large-wristed style; he described himself when I met him as an "ol' Texas country boy."

Like other stores across the country, Neiman-Marcus had months earlier received extensive corporate guidelines on the look of its advertisements, window displays, and counters for the launching of the new scent. Some enthusiastic local deviation from the party line was to be counted on, just the same. The last time I saw Ira Levy, he had been still trying, at the eleventh hour, to rein in possible excess. "I remember I had lunched with Mrs. Lauder at the Carlyle," Levy said a couple of days before she left for Dallas. "We were looking at this floral arrangement. She said she wanted that feeling for the new fragrance—a whole garden in a vase. You know the way those florists at the Carlyle can do it— African violets wired to four-foot-high stems, that kind of thing. First, I thought, Isn't this wonderful? Then I thought, But in some parts of the country they won't know how to do it with—let's just say with any great splendor. It'll turn out dusty. It'll look horrible. Then we had that sales meeting in Paris and a luncheon at the Pré Catelan. There was this *humongous* great flower arrangement, with pink ribbons trailing about! It was terrible—the confirmation of my worst fears. I'm still trying to get things back to the original simplicity. Since the ad, the music, things have really come together for me. But I'm still nervous about how the show will play on the road."

A HUNDRED and fifty beauty advisers eating breakfast while dressed in smocks of audaciously pink polyester bengaline cast quite a glow. It fought to a standoff the banquet ghosts in the Grand Ballroom of the Hotel Adolphus, in downtown Dallas. The women gathered for this first of a nationwide burst of "Beautiful Breakfasts" represented the original Nei- man-Marcus, adjacent to the hotel, and also Neiman-Marcus stores in malls in suburban NorthPark and Prestonwood and in Fort Worth. (The breakfast was one of only a handful that would be honored by Mrs. Lauder's presence, the others being scheduled a couple of weeks later in New York. Mostly, the events would form part of a regular pattern of instruction in selling new products, led by the training directors of an elaborate Lauder network.) Bob Tetley said that some of the Fort Worth girls had had to leave home at four-thirty that morning in order to board the bus. The breakfast group looked happy enough, unified by pink and by their valorous makeups. They were more motley than the Woodcliff Lake executives: some looked young and bubbling with ideas from hairdo magazines, while others looked older beneath their bright-dyed hair, as if the ashtrays, with their red-tinged butts, also held some dented, country-music dreams.

Each setting had an orchid and a small pink shopping bag with samples of lipstick, nail lacquer, and eau de parfum. The centerpiece on each table took a very broad stab at florally expressing the simple, spiritual theme.

"The flowers would *not* have been our choice," Monroe Alechman said gloomily, shooting his cuffs. "The Japanese would commit hara-kiri."

On a dais was the four-foot-high pink-and-gold box (known as "the exploded box," this would serve as a separate sales point in stores, away from the Lauder counter), laid out with the S.K.U.s. Next to them, on an easel, was a newcomer to the display: the forthcoming autobiography. Rather, it was a mockup of the autobiography, since the book itself was not yet in print. It was entitled *Estée: A Success Story,* and its jacket was shiny and red. (I later learned that there had been almost as much to-ing and fro-ing on the book's title as on the name of the new scent. "It was going to be 'Our Success Story,' then it was 'My Success Story,' then Mrs. Lauder said ' "*A* Success Story," that's enough,' " my informant said.) Much of the front of the book was taken up by a photograph of Estée Lauder in the poppy-print red dress and hat, standing in front of a Chinese cabinet. She wore a serene expression, and was very softly lit.

She sailed into the ballroom now, to an ovation encouraged by Tetley. She was wearing a red silk dress, a matching hat with rosette and veil, and the familiar diamond earrings and pin. I observed that the print was slightly different from the first outfit I had seen; this one had leaves, black on the red, instead of poppies.

"We suggested that it would be a good idea for Mrs. Lauder to wear a dress of a color and pattern similar to the ones on the book," Monroe Alechman said, in an undertone. "To keep tying it in, the way we do a product launch."

"This is the first appearance by Miz Lauder in any store outside home base in ten years!" Tetley said from the dais. Estée Lauder was champing at the bit; she rose happily to stand beside her mirror image on the book. Both red selves clashed somewhat with Beautiful Pink.

"Pink is shocking, blatantly impactful," Alechman said. "It is almost as powerful as red."

"Listen, girls!" Estée Lauder said after romping through the Palm Beach ladies and the two thousand flowers. "I just returned from France. I saw the show at Hubert de Givenchy, and at the end he had a bride, and—what do you know?—he'd put her in pink! I thought, How did he know I was doing pink!"

As she was dressed for it, she said, she would show them her book.

"Every one of you can be an Estée Lauder!" she continued. "I want to thank each and every one of you for wearing your pink. You're beautiful. No matter how old you are, you can always feel like a bride. Now I'm going to show you my new commercial. It's going to be on every television throughout the world!"

Willow Bay came floating out of green-dappled light on a screen, to the sound of the crooning Cohn. A hundred and fifty potential Estée Lauders sat in the darkened room resting their chin on their hands and sighing at the almost immediate end.

"Play it through again!" came Estée Lauder's voice from the dark.

One of the young women from the NorthPark table had put her orchid behind one ear. "I'd like to look like her on *my* wedding day," she said, gathering the gifts and her purse and preparing to start for work. "I liked the little girl running. I thought she was real cute."

Estée Lauder left word that waiters clearing the fast-emptying tables might keep some of the uncollected free samples for their girlfriends and their wives. Then she headed for the waiting car. "Hard work never killed anyone," she said gaily, opening her pocketbook as she settled against the cushions in the back. She took out a gold metal compact—it was one of the "Anniversary" compacts, and was monogrammed with a big, bold "E"—and tilted its mirror until she could see to correct the angle of her hat. She uncapped a postmodern lipstick tube and—deftly, as she had for countless times in her successful life—applied fresh red color to her mouth. "I just put on my dress, my hat, you see," she said, lifting one hand to give the rosette a little pat. "I call this my ready-to-go outfit. I wore it to Yasmin Ali Khan's wedding—a lovely affair. My friends said, 'Estée, how clever of you to wear red.' "

Rebecca McGreavy and Toni Hopkins flanked her; she never looks happier than with younger women whom she trusts.

"A dime out of every dollar!" Tetley was saying excitedly, swivelling around in his seat beside the car's driver, a long way up front. It seemed that cosmetics accounted for twenty-five percent of the business at Neiman-Marcus Fort Worth, and Estée Lauder alone accounted for ten percent. "That's more than Neiman-Marcus NorthPark, more than Bloomingdale's Fifty-ninth. More Estée Lauder business than any other store in the United States, during the Christmas season."

Estée Lauder listened with half an ear, looking out the window. We passed a thermometer in front of a bank; it registered a hundred and two.

"In business, you reap what you sow," Estée Lauder said, continuing along her stream of consciousness. "The Lauder family keeps plowing the profits back in. And what we gave away God always gave back to us. Gift with purchase was my idea, I was the first to think of that. I never copy. The others copy me. . . . Skin Perfecting Creme is magnificent. . . . My new bath fragrance, we haven't got the name yet, but it will be green. Something like Green Water, but not Green Water."

Wasn't there a Green Water by Jacques Fath, someone said.

"Jacques Fath!" she shot back. "He's dead. I'm talking about Estée Lauder's Green Water."

THE long black car swung across the sparsely filled parking lot of the shopping mall, under the big Texas sky. Neiman-Marcus Fort Worth was just starting its day. Inside, the store was cool and pale. A handful of shoppers sleepwalked up and down the escalators or pushed with half-hearted clickings at racks of clothes. A full-length white mink coat with Lurex trim stood like a sentry over a scampering little cluster of plaster legs and feet on tiptoes, dressed in bright-colored pantyhose. ("Mrs. Lauder loves to go shopping," Rebecca McGreavy once told me. "Unfortunately, it's not really possible for her anymore.")

While Estée Lauder secluded herself with the fashion editor of the Fort Worth *Star-Telegram,* I wandered down a corridor into a room set aside for brides-to-be. There was a pile of dog-eared copies of *Bride's* and a sign about the Neiman-Marcus wedding service: a store employee will dress the bride and come to the ceremony with sewing kit and fresh handkerchiefs, for fifty dollars. On the wall, a photographic portrait of a blonde in a family veil fixed her and her nuptial hopes forever, beneath an aspiclike patina. She might have been twin sister to the young Josephine Esther Mentzer, of Corona, Queens (as Estée Lauder was), who sat for her portrait, with veil and glow, at the time of her wedding to Joseph Lauder. The first wedding, that is: her book would shortly reveal that she had had two weddings, to the same man, divorcing and remarrying him when Leonard Lauder was a child.

The corral of Estée Lauder counters lay at the store's strategic heart and was today a blaze of pink smocks, pink flowers, and pink-and-gold packages.

"Estée Lauder does two million eight hundred thousand dollars in this store each year," Tetley said. Young women in pink dresses and glittering shoes were picking pink fabric flowers from dainty baskets on their arms and proffering them to passersby, who held the flowers to their noses and sniffed.

"Few things hold the fragrance well," Monroe Alechman said. "This fabric does. Feathers do. I think Yves Saint Laurent used feathers for Opium."

A man with artistically dishevelled white hair and dressed in a tuxedo with a greenish tinge was steadfastly playing "You Are So Beautiful" on the violin, over and over, competing with the Cohn rendition on a nearby video.

Alechman glanced at the musician, then looked away. "We suggest that the musician be *young*," he said in a lowered voice. "This is too down. It's missing a bounce, a lift. Reminds me of White Shoulders or Tabu."

A smock-draped customer was sitting on a high stool through it all, tilting her face trustfully to the ministrations of Riba Gregg, a makeup artist at the Lauder counter.

"She comes in twice a year for us to do the new color story with her," Riba Gregg said, standing over the woman and flicking at her cheeks with a soft-haired brush dipped in blush.

The woman gave a self-conscious smile and nod.

"She knows what happened for her in her business after she changed her look," Riba Gregg said firmly.

The woman nodded again. "Everything I hoped for," she said.

Riba Gregg stepped back, surveyed her work with satisfaction, then turned away to a file. She pulled out a big chart with lots of schematic faces of women and a record of what her clients had bought on past visits.

"Got your neck cream? Your eye cream? Be sure to use your eye cream. You using the polisher at least twice a week?"

It was agreed that the woman could wait to replenish her nourishing cream until the new Skin Perfecting Creme came in.

At a signal, the violinist stopped. The pink smocks clapped, some customers looked bemused, as Estée Lauder came down among them on the escalator, radiant in her hat. The violinist tucked his instrument under his chin and, with a gallant sweep of the bow, launched into "You Are So Beautiful." She listened, with cocked head.

"Skin Perfecting Creme," she began when the music had stopped. "Tell your customers, a moisturizer and a firmer. . . . The perfume is magnificent, the cologne is lovely. Try to sell the perfume first. . . . This is my book. Gift with purchase was my idea. Even the banks are copying me now."

She rounded the end of the counter, beckoning to the several dozen pink-smocked women, who squeezed behind the counter with her for a group photograph. She stood, a patch of red in a sea of pink, pushing some samples a few inches along the countertop, then folding her hands and resting them on the glass. The women chattered, giggled, shuffled, and grinned, jostling around her like birds on a perch.

"Y'all behave yourselves, you girls. This is my boss lady, you hear?" Tetley said, joshing and giving a laugh.

"Don't take me with my mouth open," Estée Lauder told the photographer.

In the car, bound for the next store, Estée Lauder was clearly enjoying herself.

"It's all coming back to me," she said. "I used to go from Corpus Christi to San Antonio by bus. Sometimes eight hours, ten hours in the bus, all over South Texas. I built my business slowly. People say I'm lucky. They don't know how hard I've worked."

She looked thoughtful for a moment, almost sad. She glanced over at Toni Hopkins and gave her an affectionate pat. She touched the gold pin, shaped like a wheat sheaf, in Toni Hopkins' lapel. "I gave her that," she said.

Estée Lauder's connection with Neiman-Marcus is one of the longest ties of her career. For years, her products have been in the store's Christmas catalogue, famous for its fantasy and excess.

"What was it they did that year—a swimming pool filled with Aramis?" she asked.

"Surely it was a bathtub, and it was filled with Azurée," someone said.

It was Stanley Marcus, now chairman emeritus of Neiman-Marcus, who, with phenomenal skills in selling and publicizing, built the regional department store founded in 1907 by his father and aunt into a world-famous institution. Stanley Marcus's son, Richard, remains chairman and chief executive officer of what has grown to be a twenty-two-store chain, but the business was sold in 1964 to what is now the Carter Hawley Hale group, which also owns Bergdorf Goodman.

"I'm still sorry the family had to sell out," Estée Lauder said. Families with control of corporations as large as Estée Lauder are a very small group throughout the world. Estée Lauder first did business at Neiman-Marcus in 1948. "Two feet of space they gave me. It was New Year's, I did a radio interview. 'Start the year with a new face,' that's what I said, and I said, 'How does a cream know if it's dark outside?' There I was in the store first thing that morning. The people kept coming in, I touched their faces. I wore a hat with a pink rose. I always wore a hat. One woman, she says, 'Does this lipstick wear off?' So I said, 'Madam, if this lipstick never wore off I'd be out of business!'" She roared with laughter, slapped her knee, lifted her hand and set her hat straight. "I ran out of lipstick, and I said, 'Sell the tester! Go ahead and sell the tester!' Stanley Marcus must have heard there was some woman selling and selling, and he came down from his office to see. He saw us selling, talking, touching one woman's face, and ten other customers standing around."

Tetley was turning round again, his arm crooked over the back of the front seat, and he was laughing. "Estée Lauder is a company run by people who really know this business," he said. "Ninety-five percent of the fine companies have been bought up now. By drug companies, mostly. Federal regulations were eating into their easy profits. So these boys saw big profits in the cosmetic industry. They move in, do a lot of advertising, and try to get their money out fast. Eli Lilly bought Elizabeth Arden, Squibb bought Lanvin–Charles of the Ritz, Warner-Lambert bought Richard Hudnut, Sterling Drug bought Dorothy Gray, and Colgate-Palmolive bought Helena Rubinstein."

"These people, they don't know about the cosmetic business," Estée Lauder said, interrupting him. "They don't care about people. We're a cosmetic business run by people who know the cosmetic business."

The car had stopped at the porte cochère of another Neiman-Marcus. Everyone got out and stood in a hot, dry breeze, looking in at windows with mannequins in bridal gowns and foot-high bottles of Beautiful.

The store manager had come out to greet the party. "I think Raymond did a good job, don't you?" he asked, referring to his window-display artist.

Here they had hired a harpist—a pale-skinned, pale-haired young woman dressed in a pink crinoline-style dress. Her arms waved back and forth like seaweed as she twingled out "You Are So Beautiful." (For variety, on her music stand there were arrangements of "You Light Up My Life" and "Come, Thou Almighty King.") Applauding pink-smocked women and pink shopping bags stood shoulder to shoulder in ranks. There was Willow Bay on her easel, and an easel advertising Coco,

Chanel's new-season entry in the great fragrance stakes. "The New Heroine" and her red gloves taunted Lancôme's "Colours with Sophisticated Folly" across the aisle. Here were Princess Marcella Borghese's mud treatments, and the "anti-aging breakthrough," from the company called Clarins. And here were fragrant ovals of bath soap, and hairbrushes, and special creams to cure the stretch marks left by pregnancies and diets; rose-printed shower bonnets and curler covers; cosmetic purses; apricot satin eyeshades; and full-face masks of jelly-filled translucent plastic (to heat or cool), with slits for eyes, nose, and mouth. There were ornate perfume atomizers, with little nets around rubber bulbs. And there were all the fragrances so carefully positioned in the market in previous years, now crowded half-forgotten on a single countertop tray.

A broad opening (separate from the entrance that the Lauder party had used) gave onto the cloistered passage of the mall. The passage was lined with small stores, like a European village, but a village sealed off beyond heat, dust, rain, or time. A shining new car was parked at a carefree angle next to the storefront of a travel agent and a sign reading "Compliments of W. O. Bankston, Lincoln-Mercury-Merkur." Except for an occasional tapping of heels down the passageway and the distant plucking of the harp, it was very quiet.

Two women in pink smocks came out of Neiman-Marcus and turned back to face the display windows flanking the opening. Here the absent Raymond had really gone to town. Two mannequins in blond wigs, elaborately embroidered wedding gowns, and top-heavy white-veiled Edwardian-style millinery seemed to be wading ankle-high through billows of gauze. Everywhere there were showers of petals, giant bottles, and sparkling gilt letters spelling "BEAUTIFUL."

"Oh, my! Isn't it . . ." the first pink smock said.

"Beautiful," said the other, and they both began to giggle.

Next door, the front of an electronics store called Video Concepts gaped like Ali Baba's cave. Inside, twenty television sets, all tuned to the same soap opera, flickered in silence where they roosted one on top of the next; all up and down the row, a heavily made-up young couple conducted a wordy quarrel in a king-size bed. On a large TV screen to the right of the entrance there was showing some sort of documentary about a primitive tribe. An elder with gray-black skin and with a bone through his nose was talking earnestly in his own language into the camera while a trickle of white subtitles ran across his chest. On an even larger screen, to the left, a commercial for Kraft salad dressing was on: a lava flow of orange rippled from an enormous bottle onto a jungle of greens. Three small Chicano boys in striped T-shirts and sneakers came quietly down the passage and stood side by side, silently staring at the slow orange flow. The tallest child hooked a fraternal arm over the shoulders of the smallest, who wore a "Reagan-Bush" button almost as big as his head. The trio wheeled for a moment to watch the other screen, where some naked tribesman could now be seen stalking something in the bush, and then turned back to the left-hand screen.

Estée Lauder came out of Neiman-Marcus in her ready-to-go red, accompanied by the store manager. She paused; then she also turned her back on the mall, to stand looking through the glass at the two brides. The three boys went right on facing in the opposite direction—their shoulder blades, under the T-shirts, were sharp as little wings—and gazed unblinkingly as a mammoth Snickers bar snapped in two and began to ooze caramel glaciers over peanut rocks.

"Aren't these divine?" one of the pink smocks said, of the brides.

The tribal elder was looking miserable. "White man came with guns," the white word trickle read. "Make noise like thunder. Eat us up. We say, 'Oh, this is cannibal sky-spirit.' "

The second pink smock said that each of the wedding dresses cost ten thousand dollars.

"They're a real fantasy," the store manager said.

Estée Lauder was using the window glass as a mirror, smoothing her skirt and checking on the angle of her hat. A number of customers had gathered inside the store and were waiting with the beauty advisers, their voices a distant feminine buzz.

"For ten thousand dollars, you want a real fantasy," Estée Lauder said.

"Bye! Bye!"

"Thanks a lot, girls!"

"Bye!"

"Don't forget to buy my book!"

Waving, signing, selling, smiling. Yet another Neiman-Marcus, and a very long day.

"Hard work never killed anyone," she said again, heading back to her hotel. "Everyone loves a winner, though. You always have to smile. Smile and the world smiles with you, cry and you cry alone—it's true what they say. I found that out after Joe died."

Tetley was looking pleased.

"We need more of this impact-type stuff," he said. "Gets the stores all excited."

ASIDE from the rosy hubbub around the Lauder counters the next morning, the original, granddaddy Neiman-Marcus in downtown Dallas was very calm. A woman with hard-worn features under black-dyed hair was sitting in the precious-jewelry department chatting with the salesman and picking out some purchases. In the hat department, a man was looking over a display of Panama hats hanging on hooks up the wall; they seemed to skim out in chalk-pale formation, like a flight of geese.

Rebecca McGreavy was looking reverent. A team from one of the national television networks had shown up and was making Estée Lauder's eyes and lipstick shine in the camera light as she stood poised at the top of the stairs.

"They just told us to get here and shoot as much footage as we could," said the team's correspondent, a curly-haired young man in blazer and cowboy boots. "Sure is a change from covering hurricanes."

Estée Lauder, in her red net coif, looked out over the sea of loyal pink smocks and came slowly downstairs, smiling to left and right.

"Gloria Swanson," the curly-haired man said under his breath.

Customers came into her presence with boxes of Beautiful for her to sign, in gold. ("The saleswomen call their most *special* customers to let them know Mrs. Lauder will be here," a Neiman-Marcus aide said. "We would never advertise it in the newspapers.")

"You bought three?" Estée Lauder said to a customer. "That's wonderful. But you should buy it by the dozen, for Christmas."

The cameraman and the sound recordist crouched next to some pink azaleas, silently recording the stream of consciousness as it unfurled. The correspondent stood twirling a pencil between his fingers some way off, looking amused.

"You can keep on playing 'You Are So Beautiful,' " she told the pale harpist, who had been hired again for today. "It's my song."

A triumphal exit to the waiting limousine was forestalled by a flurry near the Panama hats and the appearance of Stanley Marcus at the top of the stairs. He had a squarish, white-bearded head and a short, roundish figure dressed in a three-piece gray suit, with the red rosette of the Légion d'Honneur (for service to French fashion) in his lapel. For the camera and for posterity, Stanley Marcus and Estée Lauder greeted each other with an embrace. It was wonderfully done—a pair of elderly merchant monarchs who had tested each other's titanic shrewdness for decades formally exchanging a kiss of peace.

Next, Marcus and his son were hosts of a kind of state luncheon for

Estée Lauder and Beautiful. A hundred and fifty local society ladies cooed conversationally, with their hot-pink shopping bags of gift-wrapped samples (2.5 ounces of Beautiful eau de parfum and 3.3 ounces of Lauder for Men cologne) propped against the legs of the restaurant's Louis XIV–style chairs.

Marcus's youngest brother, Lawrence, a retired executive of the family store, told the women at his table about having his portrait painted by an artist famous for his silk screens of American Indians on Hermès scarves. "The interesting thing about him is he's a mystic," he said.

"I'm interested in mysticism myself," said Juanita Miller, the wife of one of Dallas's great tycoons. ("We own some shopping centers," she had told me when I was describing the previous day's progress through the malls.) She said she needed a portrait of herself to hang in the new symphony hall.

"My little boy would like to speak to your husband," a dark-haired woman said to Juanita Miller, from her place across the table. "It's for some kind of merit badge—he's a Boy Scout, he's twelve years old. He says he wants to be a developer when he grows up, like Mr. Miller."

Stanley Marcus, over at his table, rose from his seat, at Estée Lauder's left, and made a speech, keeping his hands in his trouser pockets and choosing his words with care. "Estée is an amazing woman," he said. "She saw her opportunity in what was at the time a field of giants."

I caught up with him later, when—after being exposed to the real Estée Lauder, to *Estée: A Success Story,* and to thirty seconds' worth of Willow Bay—his guests were drifting away.

"Estée Lauder came in without an introduction, forty years ago," Marcus said. "Barged her way in. She was a cyclone on the selling front. She'd outsell *me* any day. Great salespeople all have the same quality: they believe in the integrity of their product, and they believe in themselves. The important thing in selling, I always say, is satisfaction. If I sell you something that gives you satisfaction, you will come back. I hate to think that I might be the last of a species, one of the last remaining real merchants, but it's probably true. In my time, the important thing was being able to sell. Today, it's all computerization of goods. And instead of running one or two stores people have twenty-two, or a hundred and eighty. Human beings can't cope with that, and they have to turn to computers. Computers can do wonderful things. They can tell you how many lipsticks or umbrellas you have in stock. But computers can't tell you whether you are satisfying people."

I asked how he liked the name Beautiful.

"Well, you can't get much more generic than that," he said, looking wry. "Will it be a success, though? No question. There's too much invested in it for it not to be. The old idea 'A good product will find its own level' isn't enough anymore in a market as sophisticated as the American market. Marketing a fragrance is just like marketing an automobile. And Estée Lauder has always had a wonderful sense of timing. She has always known how to anticipate what the public wants."

I said that Leonard Lauder's instincts seemed sound as well.

"That is one of the greatest of all her accomplishments," Marcus said. "To be as strong a woman as she is, to be the mother of an equally strong son, and not have the two of them kill each other."

Young women in ladylike silk dresses were gathering up the unclaimed pink shopping bags. Marcus pulled a watch from a fob pocket, then crooked a finger at one of the young women.

"Better let me have one of those for my wife," he said, snapping the watch's case shut.

"Just one?" said the young woman.

"Better let me have a couple."

·  ·  ·

"YOU know that what I say is common sense," Estée Lauder often tells her employees or her customers. Her giant international empire might be said to rest on two commandments: "Trust me" and "Eat." Only a few days after launching Beautiful in Dallas, Estée Lauder was back in New York launching a new men's scent, called Tuscany, with a well-attended Italian dinner at La Colonna. Many of the women were dressed like figures in Renaissance paintings, in black or red. Norman Parkinson was in black velvet and was escorting Nancy Tuck Gardiner, of *Town & Country,* in strapless red. Andy Warhol had his red spectacle frames and his black-and-white badger-striped hair. The American ambassador to Italy was there, and the chairman of Bloomingdale's. There were thirty-five general managers of Estée Lauder International, visiting from all over for a general meeting: men, for the most part, with blown-dry hair and freshly scented jaws. There were Estée, Leonard, and Evelyn Lauder, and a full court muster of Bob Barnes, Ira Levy, Rebecca McGreavy, Alvin Chereskin, and June Leaman.

"I'm really into girls' scents," Warhol told me, in his whispery voice, when speeches were over and the food was served. His face was like a woodland creature's, under a stork's nest of hair. He had not yet heard of Beautiful. "Beautiful?" he said. "Are you serious? That's the name? I love it. Are they giving a party for it? When? I have about ten bottles of Poison, yes. I love it. And Coco. I have one bottle of that, but I want to get another bottle before I open it. Obsession, that's *great.* " He had been able to count five hazy figures in Calvin Klein's controversial group-sex advertisement, he said.

Fred Langhammer—an Odin-like figure with close-cropped blond hair and pale-blue eyes, freshly arrived from his native Munich to serve Leonard Lauder as his second-in-command—now engaged the artist in talk about tycoons they both knew, in Germany and Japan. Langhammer had worked for many years in the Far East, where he made great strides in selling Clinique to the Japanese. Traditionally, the Japanese cosmetic market, like the European, is more for skin-treatment products than the American market, which is still predominantly for colors—lipstick, eye-shadow, and so forth. And fragrances, which make up more than half of all cosmetic business in this country, account for only three percent of Japan's. This is said to be because the Japanese eat a predominantly vegetarian diet, and so their bodies smell more sweet.

Like Leonard Lauder, it seemed, Langhammer took his ease with a certain purposefulness. He was a martial artist and had climbed in the Himalayas. The previous year, he had gone with his son to Africa, and they had slept in the bush without a tent. "We built a big fire. We could hear the lions and hyenas roar," he said, in his German-accented voice.

Andy Warhol looked alarmed. "How old is your son?" he asked.

"He is nine now. Then he was eight," Langhammer said.

Across the table, Evelyn Lauder was talking animatedly about how Beautiful got its name.

"I was the one who fought," she was saying. "I was the one who said, 'Let's *do* it!' And that's a true story. I really pushed. Leonard was in the bathtub, and I took the soap and wrote 'Beautiful' across the mirror in that big script, like the old Revlon script."

"How do I get a sample?" Andy Warhol asked.

Evelyn Lauder produced from her evening purse the refillable quarter-ounce gold perfume spray. He fumbled with the cap, then sprayed some on one hand and behind one ear.

"You can keep that," she told him.

I asked Warhol how he felt about looking older.

"Wrinkles, you mean? Oh, I hate that. I go for collagen treatments once a month."

I quoted Colette, who said that a woman, at least, must after a certain age choose between her face and her figure.

Warhol said that that was true—that fat women didn't need to worry about wrinkles. "I like old women to be skinny, though," he said. "Really skinny. Like toothpicks."

As people were beginning to get up and leave, Warhol suggested that he and I should found our own cosmetic company. "With stuff you have to keep in the refrigerator, then throw out at the end of the week," he said. "Like butter. I always use butter on my hands."

ONE noontime the next week, Estée Lauder stopped traffic on Fifth Avenue at Fiftieth Street by crossing on foot in her red-and-black ready-to-go, accompanied by Willow Bay in her bridal gown and train. They had paid a brief surprise visit to the beauty advisers at Saks, and were en route to the official Beautiful Luncheon, in the restaurant downstairs at Rockefeller Center. Estée Lauder came down one flight of steps—toward what is the skating rink in winter—and posed for photographers, one arm lifted high above her head, spraying the Indian-summer air with Beautiful. Some models stood behind her, dressed in amazing flower costumes. Beside the gazellelike creature wearing a skirt hoop of white picket fence and a hat like a pot of narcissi on her head, even the ready-to-go seemed to pale. And Willow Bay—who had been helped into her wedding togs several dozen times by now, for photographs, filming, publicity, and a Chicago fashion show—was beginning to look a little like Miss Havisham.

Estée Lauder descended the next flight of stairs to join the guests gathered on the patio under special bright-pink sun umbrellas. A young woman dressed as a rose, her face like a dewdrop at the center of a two-foot-high bud of padded pink satin, followed her with her eyes. "It didn't seem this heavy when I put it on," she said.

The model standing on her other side looked very young and very bored. She showed an exquisite profile under a swooping four-foot circle of creamy pleated silk. I asked if she was an Oriental poppy.

"I've no idea," she said, with a heartfelt sigh.

The notion of inviting "New York's Hundred Most Beautiful Women" to the luncheon had been mooted but swiftly rejected, as too likely to offend uninvited friends. Instead, the serviceable guest list included people from Saks (which co-sponsored the event), from the Parks Council (which benefitted), and from the advertising and magazine-publishing worlds, and also women friends of Evelyn Lauder; the dress designers Mary McFadden and Kasper; the sociable Andy Warhol and Jerome Zipkin, the man-about-town; an angelic-looking five-year-old, who turned out to be the Botticelli child's double; and the Lauder court muster. Many of the last were dressed wholly or partly, and with various levels of enthusiasm, in pink. ("Phyllis and I have decided that pink is really the new neutral," Rebecca McGreavy had told me not long before.)

Alvin Chereskin, in a pink shirt, was standing among the pink umbrellas with head tilted back, looking up. Tourists leaned over the parapet above the sunken space where he stood. The ring of their down-turned, curious faces hung hovering over the bright-colored gathering like faces watching lords and ladies from medieval battlements in a Book of Hours. Above them, sun rays ricocheted from the gilded statue of Prometheus. Higher yet, a rank of multicolored flags rippled out from tall poles against an azure sky. A fluffy white cloud drifted by.

"Gorgeous," Chereskin said. "The luck of the Lauders, you see."

It was after her guests were at table that Estée Lauder made her entrance, slow-stepping and smiling, with *Estée: A Success Story* held like a sacred tome in front of her, at bosom height. Willow Bay, wearing an expression both modest and ironic, followed some paces behind in her veil and gown.

"I kept putting it on this lady in Palm Beach, then on another,"

Estée Lauder told the group. She ran through the rich aunt and the imitative banks. "I didn't get there by dreaming about it! Hoping for it. Wishing for it. I got there by working for it!" she said.

"Everyone loves a winner," Kasper said, under cover of the applause.

Willow Bay and Jerome Zipkin were paired at Estée Lauder's table. I looked over and saw the two profiles turned to each other, close and sociable, as if they were weaving plots: to the right was the porcelain cameo of the beautiful young woman, pink-washed from the light of her rosebud crown and half-concealed by a slanting scrim of white wedding veil; to the left were the cynical, worldly-wise features of the man, who had spent several times her time on earth lifting his fork and gossiping at thousands of tables like today's.

At the end of the meal, Bob Barnes was standing like a rock in a flowing stream of Beautiful Pink shopping bags filled with perfume samples and sweeping up the stairs, out into the world. He had his hand flat on his heart, as if on alert to pledge allegiance to the flag. Reports of early reorders from Neiman-Marcus, he said, were more than encouraging. "It's going to be big numbers," he said. "It's blowing out."


THE morning after Saks Fifth Avenue's double-page advertisement for Beautiful ran in *The New York Times,* on the last Sunday in September, Estée Lauder was to visit the store. The appearance was not advertised to the public.

"Mrs. Lauder has confirmed the visit," an executive of the store told me. "It is part of her schedule for today, and that is as official as it gets."

During the weekend, Estée Lauder had made some store visits that had been truly unexpected. Attended only by Rebecca McGreavy and her security man, she had descended for spot checks on the Lauder counters at

Bloomingdale's and Macy's. At the first, she had been roused to indignation by the discovery of a beauty adviser using lavish amounts of Skin Perfecting Creme. Wasting the product in the course of demonstrating to customers is a hobbyhorse with her. "We're in the selling business, not the makeup business," she often says. At Macy's, the visit had unmasked a more heinous crime: a model hired to spray Giorgio scent, a competitor, had been violating the air rights around the Estée Lauder space.

Saks had pulled out all the stops: flowers, smocks, cocktail music on a white piano, big bottles in the window, videos with the indefatigable bride. (The commercial had made its television debut some days before, with the store tag urging customers to Macy's.)

Bob Barnes looked at the display with satisfaction. "It really pops," he said.

The pink plastic ripples of Beautiful testers kept cropping up, like Trojan horses, on the counter space of the competition. Young men in dinner jackets and young women in shocking-pink dresses (obtained at Lord & Taylor, because Saks had nothing suitable in stock) strolled and wheeled around the aisles with basketfuls of scented pink fabric flowers on their arms.

"Ladies!" one young man sang out. "Estée Lauder is coming! Mrs. Lauder, spraying today!"

A young woman named Mona Stack, as skinny as a whippet, with a cap of straight blond hair, stood mechanically handing out the flowers to passersby.

"This work? I do it when I'm broke," she said to me. "I have to pay the rent." Her hand dipped into her basket and handed over another scented flower. "I think it's nice when they have the men as well. I think the ladies like them coming up to them. Are you familiar with Decadence? I did the promotion for Decadence as well. They had the guys in tuxedos for that, too."

Estée Lauder arrived, slid around the counter end, and moved things here and there. She started off with some preliminary arm-high spraying; it seemed styled after the benedictory sprinklings of a Pope. A crowd had gathered, and it thickened by the minute, as if ants had got word of a crumb.

"Set up stanchions, quick!" someone said, and Estée Lauder was framed behind her counter by chromium posts and sausages of velvet-covered rope. A line formed all down the length of the counter and started slowly shuffling past her.

"Step right up!" rang the voices. "Estée Lauder! Giving away free samples! At the counter right now!"

A youth in a dinner jacket gently tucked the hand of a fat woman under his arm and escorted her to the end of the slow-moving line.

"More petals!" someone stage-whispered. "We need more petals up front."

Estée Lauder was dressed in her red-with-black-leaf-print dress and hat. Around her, the counter was a dazzle of pink and gold and sparkling light. Many of the women looked shy and humble as they drew near for her to spray them on the right hand. She handed them first a little pink card with a vial of Beautiful on it, then a little green card with a vial of Lauder for Men. "This is for you," she murmured as she bestowed the pink. "And this is for the man in your life," she murmured with the green.

The women grew fidgety as their turn drew near; they checked their appearance in mirrors, got out their pocket combs.

Barnes stood planted among a little semicircle of executives on the marble floor some yards away. With his folded arms and his big gold ring, he was a timeless figure, looking on as Estée Lauder gave her benedictory *pffft-pffft*, her twin murmured phrases, like a celebrant at Mass. The phrases took their place in a symphony: women's voices, the tinkling of the white piano, the market cries of the basket people, Cohn on the video. The air was thick with Beautiful.

Two gray-haired old women ambled off, stowing their samples in capacious bags and waving their wrists under their nostrils.

"It's a little . . ." one began.

"Pungent," said the other.

A young woman was advancing slowly through the crowd, jerkily pushing a stroller with a sleeping child in it.

"I know the information desk is in here somewhere," she said. "Today, of all days, I'm supposed to meet a friend."

The toddler was slumped oblivious in the stroller sling as it passed the knee-high shelves of bright-pink boxes, the gold letters spelling out "ESTÉE LAUDER" and "BEAUTIFUL." Light from the cabinet shone on a pair of round pink cheeks and a small mouth bubbling with some far-off dream.

"They all said I looked prettier than my picture," Estée Lauder said after she had called a halt. "Of course, *my* friends would never wait on line like that."

She got into her limousine and made for Macy's.

"They all said they used my products," she said. She gave a laugh. "Some of 'em didn't look so hot."

Rebecca McGreavy said that everyone in the world wanted to interview Mrs. Lauder now.

"It's because I'm the only one left," Estée Lauder said cheerily, adjusting the angle of her hat. "They think I'm going to drop dead soon."

Even on a Monday, Herald Square was teeming. Crowds crisscrossed the broad sidewalks in front of Macy's windows, trampling reader-and-adviser flyers and dodging the cartons of three-card-monte shills. Every one of the Broadway windows had been dedicated to the Beautiful idea; it would be held over for a second week, too. Within each window in the line, mannequins with big fake jewels and black cocktail dresses stood frozen in cell-like rooms with padded walls of pink bengaline. The fat gold letters of "ESTÉE LAUDER" and "BEAUTIFUL" rested on mirrored floors alongside anarchically downed chandeliers. Could this be Beautiful's darker, riskier, more decadent side?

"Say, they've got *some* traffic in here," Bob Barnes said as Estée Lauder and her entourage forded Macy's main floor. She took up a position—standing in front of her counter, for a change—and once again set to with her spraying and her murmured distributions of pink and green. An enormous crowd gathered immediately, scarcely needing the urging of another lively troupe of dinner-jacketed men and basket women that they should "step right up." A queue quickly formed all down the length of the long bay of counters. Women in pink smocks stood inside the ring of counters, smiling red smiles on the women who were shuffling slowly past them. Other pink smocks peeked out at the procession from a vantage point behind big glass dramming urns filled with amber-colored Private Collection, White Linen, Cinnabar, and Estée Super Perfume. On they came: a teen-ager as thin as a shoelace, all in black, with purple hair; a woman with an eight-months-pregnant belly; an old woman with a Job Lot Trading Company shopping bag, leaning on her cane; black women; white women; women in polyester pants, with spectacles on plastic chains; a woman chewing gum, and another eating ice cream from a little cup; women speaking Haitian French, and Korean, and two friends speaking Arabic and wearing the chador. Eagerly, each one drew closer to the woman in the red hat, the magic vials of pink and green. They stepped to join her in a ring of scented drops that danced and sparkled, vanished, then—at a Lauder touch on the spray-through cap—were tirelessly replaced.

A NOTE ON THE TYPE

This book was set in a digitized version of Bodoni, named after its designer, Giambattista Bodoni (1740–1813), a celebrated Italian scholar and printer. Bodoni planned his type especially for use on the more smoothly finished papers that came into vogue late in the eighteenth century and drew his letters with a mechanical regularity that is readily apparent on comparison with the less formal old style. Other characteristics that will be noted are the square serifs without fillet and the marked contrast between the light and heavy strokes.

Composed by
The Haddon Craftsmen, Inc.,
Scranton, Pennsylvania

Printed and bound by
R.R. Donnelley & Sons,
Harrisonburg, Virginia

Designed by Julie Duquet